The Collected Works

James Allen

DIAMOND BOOKS

www.diamondbooks.in

© Publisher

Publisher	:	**Diamond Pocket Books (P) Ltd.**
		X-30, Okhla Industrial Area, Phase-II
		New Delhi-110020
Phone	:	011-40712200
E-mail	:	wecare@diamondbooks.in
Website	:	www.diamondbooks.in
Edition	:	2024

The Collected Works

By - *James Allen*

About the Author

James Allen (1864–1912) was a British philosophical writer known primarily for his work on self-help and self-improvement. Also renowned for his influential works on personal development, character building, and the power of thought in shaping one's destiny. Allen is considered a pioneer in the realm of motivational and spiritual literature, offering timeless wisdom that continues to inspire readers around the world.

James Allen's writing is characterized by its simplicity, clarity, and profound insight. His works are often written in a meditative, almost poetic style, designed to provoke deep reflection. He believed that thoughts are the foundation of personal reality, a theme he explored extensively in his books. Allen's language is calm and instructive, focusing on moral and ethical improvement rather than intellectual complexity. His prose often conveys an underlying sense of compassion and earnestness, emphasizing that spiritual and material well-being are achievable through inner transformation.

Allen's works are deeply influenced by New Thought philosophy, emphasizing the law of attraction and the idea that our thoughts manifest in the physical world. His approach is direct, making complex spiritual ideas accessible. His sentences are concise, often designed to be memorable aphorisms, and his books contain practical advice on how to cultivate virtues such as patience, kindness, and diligence.

He stresses universal truths and the importance of self-discipline, mindfulness, and a strong moral character. His writing encourages self-examination, urging readers to take responsibility for their thoughts, actions, and ultimate destiny.

Allen's most famous book is *As a Man Thinketh* (1903), a work that encapsulates his core philosophy: that thoughts shape our reality. It remains a classic in the self-help genre, still widely read today for its timeless message about the transformative power of thought.

James Allen authored numerous books during his lifetime, focusing on self-help, spiritual development, and the power of thought. Here is a list of all the known books authored by him:

1. *From Poverty to Power* (1901)
2. *All These Things Added* (1903)
3. *Byways of Blessedness* (1904)
4. *Out from the Heart* (1904)
5. *The Life Triumphant* (1908)
6. *The Mastery of Destiny* (1909)
7. *The Way of Peace* (1907)
8. *The Path of Prosperity* (1907)
9. *The Heavenly Life* (1904)
10. *Morning and Evening Thoughts* (1909)
11. *Man: King of Mind, Body and Circumstance* (1909)
12. *Above Life's Turmoil* (1910)
13. *Eight Pillars of Prosperity* (1911)
14. *Foundation Stones to Happiness and Success* (1913, posthumous)
15. *The Shining Gateway* (1915, posthumous)
16. *Men and Systems* (1914, posthumous)
17. *Poems of Peace* (1913, posthumous)
18. *James Allen's Book of Meditations for Every Day in the Year* (1913, posthumous)
19. *Light on Life's Difficulties* (1912)
20. *The Divine Companion* (1919, posthumous)

These books emphasize the importance of thought, ethical living, and self-responsibility, forming a rich body of work in the self-improvement genre.

Preface

"Foundational self-help teachings compiled."

"The Collected Works of James Allen" is a comprehensive anthology that brings together the profound writings of one of the early pioneers of self-help and personal development literature. This collection encapsulates his extensive body of work, showcasing his philosophical insights, motivational essays, and practical guidance on achieving personal and spiritual growth.

The collection covers various themes, including the importance of character, the pursuit of virtue, the nature of prosperity, and the quest for spiritual enlightenment. Each essay is a reflection of Allen's belief that everyone has the power to shape their destiny through conscious choices and self-mastery.

Reading "The Collected Works of James Allen" is essential for anyone seeking personal development and a deeper understanding of themselves. This anthology not only provides a comprehensive overview of Allen's philosophy but also serves as a practical guide for implementing his teachings in daily life. His emphasis on self-reflection and personal responsibility encourages readers to take charge of their thoughts and actions, fostering a mindset conducive to growth and success.

Furthermore, Allen's insights into the nature of happiness and fulfillment challenge societal norms around wealth and success, prompting readers to reconsider what it means to lead a meaningful life. By exploring the interplay between thoughts and circumstances, readers are empowered to rise above challenges and cultivate a more enriching existence.

Ultimately, this collection is not just a compilation of writings; it is a roadmap to inner peace, prosperity, and a life of purpose. For anyone interested in personal transformation and spiritual growth, *"The Collected Works of James Allen"* is an invaluable resource that offers timeless wisdom and guidance.

Contents

Man: King Of Mind, Body And Circumstance

Foreword

The problem of life consists in learning how to live. It is like the problem of addition or subtraction to the schoolboy. When mastered, all difficulty disappears, and the problem has vanished. All the problems of life, whether they be social, political, or religious, subsist in ignorance and wrong-living. As they are solved in the heart of each individual, they will be solved in the mass of men. Humanity at present is in the painful stage of "learning." It is confronted with the difficulties of its own ignorance. As men learn to live rightly, learn to direct their forces and use their functions and faculties by the light of wisdom, the sum of life will be correctly done, and its mastery will put an end to all the "problems of evil." To the wise, all such problems have ceased.

JAMES ALLEN

Within, around, above, below,
The primal forces burn and brood,
Awaiting wisdom's guidance; lo!
All their material is good:
Evil subsists in their abuse;
Good, in their wise and lawful use.

1. The inner world of thoughts

Man is the maker of happiness and misery. Further, he is the creator and perpetuator of his own happiness and misery. These things are not externally imposed; they are internal conditions. Their cause is neither deity, nor devil, nor circumstance, but *Thought.* They are the effects of deeds, and deeds are the visible side of thoughts. Fixed attitudes of mind determine courses of conduct, and from courses of conduct come those reactions called *happiness* and *unhappiness.* This being so, it follows that, to alter the reactive condition, one must alter the active thought. To exchange misery for happiness it is necessary to reverse the fixed attitude of mind and habitual course of conduct which is the cause of misery, and the reversed effect will appear in the mind and life. A man has no power to be happy while thinking and acting selfishly; he cannot be unhappy while thinking and acting unselfishly. Wheresoever the cause is, there the effect will appear. Man cannot abrogate effects, but he can alter causes. He can purify his nature; he can remould his character. There is great power in self-conquest; there is great joy in transforming oneself.

Each man is circumscribed by his own thoughts, but he can gradually extend their circle; he can enlarge and elevate his mental sphere. He can leave the low, and reach up to the high; he can refrain from harbouring thoughts that are dark and hateful, and can cherish thoughts that are bright and beautiful; and as he does his, he will pass into a higher sphere of power and beauty, will become conscious of a more complete and perfect world.

For men live in spheres low or high according to the nature of their thoughts. Their world is as dark and narrow as they conceive it to be, as expansive and glorious as their comprehensive capacity. Everything around them is tinged with the colour of their thoughts.

Consider the man whose mind is suspicious, covetous, envious. How small and mean and drear everything appears to him. Having no grandeur in himself, he sees no grandeur anywhere; being ignoble himself, he is incapable of seeing nobility in any being. Even his God is a covetous being that can be bribed, and he judges all men and women to be just as petty and selfish as he himself is, so that he sees in the most exalted acts of unselfishness only motives that are mean and base.

Consider again the man whose mind is unsuspecting, generous, magnanimous. How wondrous and beautiful is his world. He is conscious of some kind of nobility in all creatures and beings. He sees men as true, and to him they are true. In his presence the meanest forget their nature, and for the moment become like himself, getting a glimpse, albeit confused, in that temporary upliftments of a higher order of things, of an immeasurably nobler and happier life.

That small-minded, and this large-hearted, man live in two different worlds, though they be neighbours. Their consciousness embraces totally different principles. Their actions are each the reverse of the other. Their moral insight is contrary. They each look out upon a different order of things. Their mental spheres are separate, and, like two detached circles, they never mingle. The one is in hell, the other in heaven as truly as they will ever be, and death will not place a greater gulf between them than already exists. To the one, the world is a den of thieves; to the other, it is the dwelling-place of Gods. The one keeps a revolver handy, and is always on his guard against being robbed or cheated (unconscious of the fact that he is all the time robbing and cheating himself), the other keeps ready a banquet for the best. He throws open his doors to talent, beauty, genius, goodness. His friends are of the aristocracy of character. They have become a part of himself. They are in his sphere of thought, his world of consciousness. From his heart pours forth nobility, and it returns to him tenfold in the multitude of those who love him and do him honour.

The natural grades in human society - what are they but spheres of thought, and modes of conduct manifesting those spheres? The proletariat may rail against these divisions, but he will not alter or affect them. There is no artificial remedy for equalising states of thought having no natural affinity, and separated by the fundamental principles of life. The lawless and the law-abiding are eternally apart, nor is it hatred nor pride that separates them, but states of intelligence and modes of conduct which in the moral principles of things stand mutually unrelated. The rude and ill-mannered are shut out from the circle of the gentle and refined by the impassable wall of their own mentality which, though they may remove by patient self-improvement, they can never scale by a vulgar intrusion. The kingdom of heaven is not taken by violence, but he who conforms to its principles receives the password. The ruffian moves in a society of ruffians; the saint is one of an elect brethren whose communion is divine music. All men are mirrors reflecting according to their own surface. All men, looking at the world of men and things, are looking into a mirror which gives back their own reflection.

Each man moves in the limited or expansive circle of his own thoughts, and all outside that circle is non-existent to him. He only knows that which he has become. The narrower the boundary, the more convinced is the man that there is no further limit, no other circle. The lesser cannot contain the greater, and he has no means of apprehending the larger minds; such knowledge comes only by growth. The man who moves in a widely extended circle of thought knows all the lesser circles from which he has emerged, for in the larger experience all lesser experiences are contained and preserved; and when his circle impinges upon the sphere of perfect manhood, when he is fitting himself for company and communion with them of blameless conduct and profound understanding, then his wisdom will have become sufficient to convince him that there are wider circles still beyond of which he is as yet but dimly conscious, or is entirely ignorant.

Men, like schoolboys, find themselves in standards or classes to which their ignorance or knowledge entitles them. The curriculum of the sixth standard is a mystery to the boy in the first; it is outside and beyond the circle of his comprehension; but he reaches it by persistent effort and patient growth in learning. By mastering and outgrowing all the standards between, he comes at last to the sixth, and makes its learning his own; and beyond still is the sphere of the teacher. So in life, men whose deeds are dark and selfish, full of passion and personal desire, cannot comprehend those whose deeds are bright and unselfish, whose minds are calm, deep, and pure, but they can reach this higher standard, this enlarged consciousness, by effort in right doing, by growth in thought and moral comprehension. And above and beyond all lower and higher standards stand the Teachers of mankind, the Cosmic Masters, the Saviours of the world whom the adherents of the various religions worship. There are grades in teachers as in pupils, and some there are who have not yet reached the rank and position of *Master*, yet, by the sterling morality of their character, are guides and teachers; but to occupy a pulpit or rostrum does not make a man a teacher. A man is constituted a teacher by virtue of that moral greatness which calls forth the respect and reverence of mankind.

Each man is as low or high, as little or great, as base or noble as his thoughts; no more, no less. Each moves within the sphere of his own thoughts, and that sphere is his world. In that world in which he forms his habits of thought, he finds his company. He dwells in the region which harmonises with his particular growth. But he need not perforce remain in the lower worlds. He can lift his thoughts and ascend. He can pass above and beyond into higher realms, into happier habitations. When he chooses and wills he can break the carapace of selfish thought, and breathe the purer airs of a more expansive life.

2. The outer world of things

The world of things is the other half of the world of thoughts. The inner informs the outer. The greater embraces the lesser. Matter is the counterpart of mind. Events are streams of thought. Circumstances are combinations of thought, and the outer conditions and actions of others in which each man is involved are intimately related to his own mental needs and development. Man is a part of his surroundings. He is not separate from his fellows, but is bound closely to them by the peculiar intimacy and interaction of deeds, and by those fundamental laws of thought which are the roots of human society.

One cannot alter external things to suit his passing whims and wishes, but he can set aside his whims and wishes; he can so alter his attitude of mind towards externals that they will assume a different aspect. He cannot mould the actions of others towards him, but he can rightly fashion his actions towards them. He cannot break down the wall of circumstance by which he is surrounded, but he can wisely adapt himself to it, or find the way out into enlarged circumstances by extending his mental horizon. Things follow thoughts. Alter your thoughts, and things will receive a new adjustment. To reflect truly the mirror must be true. A warped glass gives back an exaggerated image. A disturbed mind gives a distorted reflection of the world. Subdue the mind, organise and tranquillise it, and a more beautiful image of the universe, a more prefect perception of the world-order will be the result.

Man has all power within the world of his own mind, to purify and perfect it; but his power in the outer world of other minds is subject and limited. This is made plain when we reflect that each finds himself in a world of men and things, a unit amongst myriads of similar units. These units do not act independently and despotically, but responsively and sympathetically. My fellow-men are involved in my actions, and they will deal with them. If what I do be a menace to them, they will adopt protective measures against me. As the human body expels its morbid atoms, so the body politic instinctively expurgates its recalcitrant members. Your wrong acts are so many wounds inflicted on this body politic, and the healing of its wounds will be your pain and sorrow. This ethical cause and effect is not different from that physical cause and effect with which the simplest is acquainted. It is but an extension of the same law; its application to the larger body of humanity. No act is aloof. Your most secret deed is invisibly reported, its good being protected in joy, its evil destroyed in pain. There is a great ethical truth in the old fable of "the Book of Life," in which every thought and deed is recorded and judged. It is because of this – that your deed belongs, not alone to yourself, but to humanity and the universe - that you are powerless to avert external effects, but are all-powerful to modify and correct internal causes; and it is also because of this that the perfecting of one's own deeds is man's highest duty and most sublime accomplishment.

The obverse of this truth – that you are powerless to obviate external things and deeds – is, that external things and deeds are powerless to injure you. The cause of your bondage as of your deliverance is within. The injury that comes to you through others is the rebound of your own deed, the reflex of your own mental attitude. *They* are the instruments, *you* are the cause. Destiny is ripened deeds. The fruit of life, both bitter and sweet, is received by each man in just measure. The righteous man is free. None can injure him; none can destroy him; none can rob him of his peace. His attitude towards men, born of understanding, disarms their power to wound him. Any injury which they may try to inflict, rebounds upon themselves to their own hurt, leaving him unharmed and untouched. The good that goes from him is his perennial fount of happiness, his eternal source of strength. Its root is serenity, its flower is joy.

The harm which a man sees in the action of another towards him – say, for instance, an act of slander – is not in the act itself, but in his attitude of mind towards it; the injury and unhappiness are created by himself, and subsist in his lack of understanding concerning the nature and power of deeds. He thinks the act can permanently injure or ruin his character, whereas it is utterly void of any such power; the reality being that the deed can only injure or ruin the doer of it. Thinking himself injured, the man becomes agitated and unhappy, and takes great pains to counteract the supposed harm to himself, and these very pains give the slander an appearance of truth, and aid rather than hinder it. All his agitation and unrest is created by his reception of the deed, and not actually by the deed itself. The righteous man has proved this by the fact that the same act has ceased to arouse in him any disturbance. He understands, and therefore ignores, it. It belongs to a sphere which he has ceased to inhabit, to a region of consciousness with which he has no longer any affinity. He does not receive the act into himself, the thought of injury to himself being absent. He lives above the mental darkness in which such acts thrive, and they can no more injure or disturb him than a boy can injure or divert the sun by throwing stones at it. It was to emphasise this that Buddha, to the end of his days, never ceased to tell his disciples that so long as the thought "I have been injured," or "I have been cheated," or "I have been insulted," could arise in a man's mind, he had not comprehended the Truth.

And as with the conduct of others, so is it with external things – with surroundings and circumstances – in themselves they are neither good nor bad, it is the mental attitude and state of heart that makes them so. A man imagines he could do great things if he were not hampered by circumstances - by want of money, want of time, want of influence, and want of freedom from family ties. In reality the man is not hindered by these things at all. He, in his mind, ascribes to them a power which they do not possess, and he submits not to them, but to his opinion about them, that is, to a weak element in his nature. The real "want" that hampers him is the *want of the right attitude of mind.* When he regards his circumstances as spurs to his resources, when he sees that his so-called "drawbacks" are the very steps up which he is to mount successfully to his achievement, then his necessity gives birth to invention, and the "hindrances" are transformed into *aids. The man* is the all-important factor. If his mind be wholesome and rightly tuned, he will not whine and whimper over his circumstances, but will rise up, and outgrow them. He who complains of his circumstances has not yet become a man, and Necessity will continue to prick and lash him till he rises into manhood's strength, and then she will submit to him. Circumstance is a severe taskmaster to the weak, an obedient servant to the strong.

It is not external things, but our thoughts about them, that bind us or set us free. We forge our own chains, build our own dungeons, take ourselves prisoners; or we loose our bonds, build our own palaces, or roam in freedom through all scenes and events. If I think that my surroundings are powerful to bind me, that thought will keep me bound. If I think that, in my thought and life, I can rise above my surroundings, that thought will liberate me. One should ask of his thoughts, "Are they leading to bondage or deliverance?" and he should abandon thoughts that bind, and adopt thoughts that set free.

If we fear our fellow-men, fear opinion, poverty, the withdrawal of friends and influence, then we are bound indeed, and cannot know the inward happiness of the enlightened, the freedom of the just; but if in our thoughts we are pure and free, if we see in life's reactions and reverses nothing to cause us trouble or fear, but everything to aid us in our progress, nothing remains that can prevent us from accomplishing the aims of our life, for then we are free indeed.

3. Habit: its slavery and its freedom

Man is subject to the law of habit. Is he then free? Yes, he is free. Man did not make life and its laws; they are eternal; he finds himself involved in them and he can understand and obey them. Man's power does not enable him to make laws of being; it subsists in discrimination and choice. Man does not create one jot of the universal conditions or laws; they are the essential principles of things, and are neither made nor unmade. He discovers, not makes, them. Ignorance of them is at the root of the world's pain. To defy them is folly and bondage. Who is the freer man, the thief who defies the laws of his country or the honest citizen who obeys them? Who, again, is the freer man, the fool who thinks he can live as he likes, or the wise man who chooses to do only that which is right?

Man is, in the nature of things, a being of habit, and this he cannot alter; but he can alter his habits. He cannot alter the law of his nature, but he can adapt his nature to the law. No man wishes to alter the law of gravitation, but all men adapt themselves to it; they use it by bending to it, not by defying or ignoring it. Men do not run up against walls or jump over precipices in the hope that the law will alter for them. They walk alongside walls, and keep clear of precipices.

Man can no more get outside the law of habit, than he can get outside the law of gravitation, but he can employ it wisely or unwisely. As scientists and inventors master the physical forces and laws by obeying and using them, so wise men master the spiritual forces and laws in the same way. While the bad man is the whipped slave of habit, the good man is its wise director and master. Not its *maker,* let me reiterate, nor yet its arbitrary commander, but its self-disciplined user, its master by virtue of knowledge grounded on obedience. He is the bad man whose habits of thought and action are bad. He is the good man whose habits of thought and action are good. The bad man becomes the good man by transforming or transmuting his habits. He does not alter the law; he alters himself; he adapts himself to the law. Instead of submitting to selfish indulgences, he obeys moral principles. He becomes the master of the lower by enlisting in the service of the higher. The law of habit remains the same, but he is changed from bad to good by his readjustment to the law.

Habit is *repetition.* Man repeats the same thoughts, the same actions, the same experiences over and over again until they are incorporated with his being, until they are built into his character as part of himself. Faculty is fixed habit. Evolution is mental accumulation. Man, today, is the result of millions of repetitious thoughts and acts. He is not readymade, he becomes, and is still becoming. His character is predetermined by his own choice. The thought, the act, which he chooses, that, by habit, he becomes.

Thus each man is an accumulation of thoughts and deeds. The characteristics which he manifests instinctively and without effort are lines of thought and action become, by long repetition, automatic; for it is the nature of habit to become, at last, unconscious, to repeat, as it were, itself without any apparent choice or effort on the part of its possessor; and in due time it takes such complete possession of the individual as to appear to render his will powerless to counteract it. This is the case with all habits, whether good or bad; when bad, the man is spoken of as being the "victim" of a bad habit or a vicious mind; when good, he is referred to as having, by nature, a "good disposition".

All men are, and will continue to be, subject to their own habits, whether they be good or bad - that is, subject to their own reiterated and accumulated thoughts and deeds. Knowing this, the wise man chooses to subject himself to good habits, for such service is joy, bliss, and freedom; while to become subject to bad habits is misery, wretchedness, slavery.

This law of habit is beneficent, for while it enables a man to bind himself to the chains of slavish practices, it enables him to become so fixed in good courses as to do them unconsciously, to instinctively do that which is right, without restraint or exertion, and in perfect happiness and freedom. Observing this automatism in life, men have denied the existence of will or freedom on man's part. They speak of him as being "born" good or bad, and regard him as the helpless instrument of blind forces.

It is true that man is the instrument of mental forces – or, to be more accurate, he is those forces – but they are not blind, and he can direct them, and redirect them into new channels. In a word, he can take himself in hand and reconstruct his habits; for though it is also true that he is born with a given character, that character is the product of numberless lives during which it has been slowly built up by choice and effort, and in this life it will be considerably modified by new experiences.

No matter how apparently helpless a man has become under the tyranny of a bad habit, or a bad characteristic - and both are essentially the same - he can, so long as sanity remains, break away from it and become free, replacing it by its opposite good habit; and when the good possesses him as the bad formerly did, there will be neither wish nor need to break from that, for its dominance will be perennial happiness, and not perpetual misery.

That which a man has formed within himself, he can break up and re-form when he so wishes and wills; and a man does not wish to abandon a bad habit so long as he regards it as pleasurable. It is when it assumes a painful tyranny over him that he begins to look for a way of escape, and finally abandons the bad for something better.

No man is helplessly bound. The very law by which he has become a self-bound slave, will enable him to become a self-emancipated master. To know this, he has but to act upon it - that is, to deliberately and strenuously abandon the old lines of thought and conduct, and diligently fashion new and better lines. That he may not accomplish this in a day, a week, a month, a year, or five years, should not dishearten and dismay him. Time is required for the new repetitions to become established, and the old ones to be broken up; but the law of habit is certain and infallible, and a line of effort patiently pursued and never abandoned, is sure to be crowned with success; for if a bad condition, a mere negation, can become fixed and firm, how much more surely can a good condition, a positive principle, become established and powerful! A man is only powerless to overcome the wrong and unhappy elements in himself *so long as he regards himself as powerless.* If to the bad habit is added the thought "I cannot" the bad habit will remain. Nothing can be overcome till the thought of powerlessness is uprooted and abolished from the mind. The great stumbling-block is not the habit itself, it is *the belief in the impossibility of overcoming it.* How can a man overcome a bad habit so long as he is convinced that it is impossible? How can a man be prevented from overcoming it when he knows that he can, and is determined to do it? The dominant thought by which man has enslaved himself is the thought "I cannot overcome my sins." Bring this thought out into the light, in all its nakedness, and it is seen to be a belief in the power of evil, with its other pole, disbelief in the power of good. For a man to say, or believe, that he cannot rise above wrong-thinking and wrong-doing, is to submit to evil, is to abandon and renounce good.

By such thoughts, such beliefs, man binds himself; by their opposite thoughts, opposite beliefs, he sets himself free. A changed attitude of mind changes the character, the habits, the life. Man is his own deliverer. He has brought about his thraldom; he can bring about his emancipation. All through the ages he has looked, and is still looking, for an external deliverer, but he still remains bound. The Great Deliverer is within; He is the Spirit of Truth; and the Spirit of Truth is the Spirit of Good; and he is in the Spirit of Good who dwells habitually in good thoughts and their effects, good actions.

Man is not bound by any power outside his own wrong thoughts, and from these he can set himself free; and foremost, the enslaving thoughts from which he needs to be delivered are – "I cannot rise," "I cannot break away from bad habits," "I cannot alter my nature," "I cannot control and conquer myself", "I CANNOT CEASE FROM SIN." All these "cannots" have no existence in the things to which they submit; they exist only in thought.

Such negations are bad thought-habits which need to be eradicated, and in their place should be planted the positive "I can" which should be tended and developed until it becomes a powerful tree of habit, bearing the good and life-giving fruit of right and happy living.

Habit binds us; habit sets us free. Habit is primarily in thought, secondarily in deed. Turn the thought from bad to good, and the deed will immediately follow. Persist in the bad, and it will bind you tighter and tighter; persist in the good, and it will take you into ever-widening spheres of freedom. He who loves his bondage, let him remain bound. He who thirsts for freedom, let him come and be set free.

4. Bodily conditions

There are today scores of distinct schools devoted to the healing of the body; a fact which shows the great prevalence of physical suffering, as the hundreds of religions, devoted to the comforting of men's minds prove the universality of mental suffering. Each of these schools has its place in so far as it is able to relieve suffering, even where it does not eradicate the evil; for with all these schools of healing, the facts of disease and pain remain with us, just as sin and sorrow remain despite of the many religions.

Disease and pain, like sin and sorrow, are too deep-seated to be removed by palliatives. Our ailments have an ethical cause deeply rooted in the mind. I do not infer by this that physical conditions have no part in disease; they play an important part as *instruments*, as factors in the chain of causation. The microbe that carried the black death was the instrument of uncleanliness, and uncleanliness is, primarily, a moral disorder. Matter is visible mind, and that bodily conflict which we call *disease* has a causal affinity to that mental conflict which is associated with sin. In his present human or self-conscious state, man's mind is continually being disturbed by violently conflicting desires, and his body attacked by morbid elements. He is in a state of mental inharmony and bodily discomfort. Animals in their wild and primitive state are free from disease because they are free from inharmony. They are in accord with their surroundings, have no moral responsibility and no sense of sin, and are free from those violent disturbances of remorse, grief, disappointment, etc., which are so destructive of man's harmony and happiness, and their bodies are not afflicted. As man ascends into the divine or cosmic-conscious state, he will leave behind and below him all these inner conflicts, will overcome sin and all sense of sin, and will dispel remorse and sorrow. Being thus restored to mental harmony, he will become restored to bodily harmony, to wholeness, health.

The body is the image of the mind, and in it are traced the visible features of hidden thoughts. The outer obeys the inner, and the enlightened scientist of the future may be able to trace every bodily disorder to its ethical cause in the mentality.

Mental harmony, or moral wholeness, makes for bodily health. I say *makes for it*, for it will not produce it magically, as it were - as though one should swallow a bottle of medicine and then be whole and free - but if the mentality is becoming more poised and restful, if the moral stature is increasing, then a sure foundation of bodily wholeness is being laid, the forces are being conserved and are receiving a better direction and adjustment; and even if perfect health is not gained, the bodily derangement, whatever it be, will have lost its power to undermine the strengthened and uplifted mind.

One who suffers in body will not necessarily at once be cured when he begins to fashion his mind on moral and harmonious principles; indeed, for a time, while the body is bringing to a crisis, and throwing off, the effects of former inharmonies, the morbid condition may appear to be intensified. As a man does not gain perfect peace immediately he enters upon the path of righteousness, but must, except in rare instances, pass through a painful period of adjustment; neither does he, with the same rare exceptions, at once acquire perfect health. Time is required for bodily as well as mental readjustment, and even if health is not reached, it will be approached.

If the mind be made robust, the bodily condition will take a secondary and subordinate place, and will cease to have that primary importance which so many give to it. If a disorder is not cured, the mind can rise above it, and refuse to be subdued by it. One can be happy, strong, and useful in spite of it. The statement so often made by health specialists that a useful and happy life is impossible without bodily health is disproved by the fact that numbers of men who have accomplished the greatest works - men of genius and superior talent in all departments - have been afflicted in their bodies, and today there are plenty of living witnesses to this fact. Sometimes the bodily affliction acts as a stimulus to mental activity, and aids rather than hinders its work. To make a useful and happy life dependent upon health, is to put matter before mind, is to subordinate spirit to body.

Men of robust minds do not dwell upon their bodily condition if it be in any way disordered - *they ignore it*, and work on, live on, as though it were not. This ignoring of the body not only keeps the mind sane and strong, but it is the best resource for curing the body. If we cannot have a perfectly sound body, we can have a healthy mind, and healthy mind is the best route to a sound body.

A sickly mind is more deplorable than a disordered body, and it leads to sickliness of body. The mental invalid is in a far more pitiable condition than the bodily invalid. There are invalids (every physician knows them) who only need to lift themselves into a strong, unselfish, happy frame of mind to discover that their body is whole and capable.

Sickly thoughts about oneself, about one's body and food, should be abolished by all who are called by the name of *man.* The man who imagines that the wholesome food he is eating is going to injure him, needs to come to bodily vigour by the way of mental strength. To regard one's bodily health and safety as being dependent on a particular kind of food which is absent from nearly every household, is to court petty disorders. The vegetarian who says he dare not eat potatoes, that fruit produces indigestion, that apples give him acidity, that pulses are poison, that he is afraid of green vegetables and so on, is demoralising the noble cause which he professes to have espoused, is making it look ridiculous in the eyes of those robust meat eaters who live above such sickly fears and morbid self-scrutinies. To imagine that the fruits of the earth, eaten when one is hungry and in need of food, are destructive of health and life is to totally misunderstand the nature and office of food. The office of food is to sustain and preserve the body, not to undermine and destroy it. It is a strange delusion - and one that must react deleteriously upon the body - that possesses so many who are seeking health by the way of diet, the delusion that certain of the simplest, most natural, and purest of viands are *bad of themselves*, that they have in them the elements of death, and not of life. One of these food-reformers once told me that he believed his ailment (as well as the ailments of thousands of others) was caused by eating bread; not by an excess of bread, but by the bread itself; and yet this man's bread food consisted of nutty, home-made, wholemeal loaves. Let us get rid of our sins, our sickly thoughts, our self-indulgences and foolish excesses before attributing our diseases to such innocent causes.

Dwelling upon one's petty troubles and ailments is a manifestation of weakness of character. To so dwell upon them in thought leads to frequent talking about them, and this, in turn, impresses them more vividly upon the mind, which soon becomes demoralised by such petting and pitying. It is as convenient to dwell upon happiness and health as upon misery and disease; as easy to talk about them, and much more pleasant and profitable to do so.

> "Let us live happily then, not hating those who hate us!
> Among men who hate us let us dwell free from hatred!
> Let us live happily then, free from ailments among the ailing!
> Among men who are ailing let us dwell free from ailments!
> Let us live happily then, free from greed among the greedy!
> Among men who are greedy let us dwell free from greed!"

Moral principles are the soundest foundations for health, as well as for happiness. They are the true regulators of conduct, and they embrace every detail of life. When earnestly espoused and intelligently understood they will compel a man to reorganise his entire life down to the most apparently insignificant detail. While definitely regulating one's diet, they will put an end to squeamishness, food-fear, and foolish whims and groundless opinions as to the harmfulness of foods. When sound moral health has eradicated self-indulgence and self-pity, all natural foods will be seen as they are - nourishers of the body, and not its destroyers.

Thus a consideration of bodily conditions brings us inevitably back to the mind, and to those moral virtues which fortify it with an invincible protection. The morally right are the bodily right. To be continually transposing the details of life from passing views and fancies, without reference to fixed principles, is to flounder in confusion; but to discipline details by moral principles is to see, with enlightened vision, all details in their proper place and order.

For it is given to moral principle alone, in their personal domain, to perceive the moral order. In them alone resides the insight that penetrates to causes, and with them only is the power to at once command all details to their order and place, as the magnet draws and polarises the filings of steel.

Better even than curing the body is to rise above it; to be its master, and not to be tyrannised over by it; not to abuse it, not to pander to it, never to put its claims before virtue; to discipline and moderate its pleasures, and not to be overcome by its pains - in a word, to live in the poise and strength of the moral powers, this, better than bodily cure, is a yet a safe way to cure, and it is a permanent source of mental vigour and spiritual repose.

5. Poverty

Many of the greatest men through all ages have abandoned riches and adopted poverty to better enable them to accomplish their lofty purposes. Why, then, is poverty regarded as such a terrible evil? Why is it that this poverty, which these great men regard as a blessing, and adopt as a bride, should be looked upon by the bulk of mankind as a scourge and a plague? The answer is plain. In the one case, the poverty is associated with a nobility of mind which not only takes from it all appearance of evil, but which lifts it up and makes it appear good and beautiful, makes it seem more attractive and more to be desired than riches and honour, so much so that, seeing the dignity and happiness of the noble mendicant, thousands imitate him by adopting his mode of life. In the other case, the poverty of our great cities is associated with everything that is mean and repulsive - with swearing, drunkenness, filth, laziness, dishonesty and crime. What, then, is the primary evil: is it poverty, or is it sin? The answer is inevitable - it is sin. Remove sin from poverty, and its sting is gone; it has ceased to be the gigantic evil that it appeared, and can even be turned to good and noble ends. Confucius held up one of his poor disciples, Yen-hwui by name, as an example of lofty virtue to his richer pupils, yet "although he was so poor that he had to live on rice and water, and had no better shelter than a hovel, he uttered no complaint. Where this poverty would have made other men discontented and miserable, he did not allow his equanimity to be disturbed." Poverty cannot undermine a noble character, but it can set it off to better advantage. The virtues of Yen-hwui shone all the brighter for being set in poverty, like resplendent jewels set in a contrasting background.

It is common with social reforms to regard poverty as the *cause* of the sins with which it is associated; yet the same reformers refer to the immoralities of the rich as being caused by their riches. Where there is a cause its effect will appear and were affluence the cause of immorality, and poverty the cause of degradation, then every rich man would become immoral and every poor man would come to degradation.

An evil-doer will commit evil under any circumstances, whether he be rich or poor, or midway between the two conditions. A right doer will do right howsoever he be placed. Extreme circumstances may help to bring out the evil which is already there awaiting its opportunity, but they cannot cause the evil, cannot create it.

Discontent with one's financial condition is not the same as poverty. Many people regard themselves as poor whose income runs into several hundreds – and in some cases several thousands of pounds a year, combined with light responsibilities. They imagine their affliction to be poverty; their real trouble is covetousness. They imagine their affliction to be poverty; their real trouble is covetousness. They are not made unhappy by poverty, but by the thirst for riches. Poverty is more often in the mind than in the purse. So long as a man thirsts for more money he will regard himself as poor, and in that sense he is poor, for covetousness is poverty of mind. A miser may be a millionaire, but he is as poor as when he was penniless.

On the other hand, the trouble with so many who are living in indigence and degradation is that they *are* satisfied with their condition. To be living in dirt, disorder, laziness, and swinish self-indulgence, revelling in foul thoughts, foul words and unclean surroundings, and to be satisfied with oneself, is deplorable. Here again, "poverty" resolves itself into a mental condition, and its solution, as a "problem", is to be looked for in the improvement of the individual from within, rather than of his outward condition. Let a man be made clean and alert within, and he will no longer be content with dirt and degradation without. Having put his mind in order, he will then put his house in order; indeed, both he and others will know that he has put himself right by the fact that he has put his immediate surroundings right. His altered heart shows in his altered life.

There are, of course, those who are neither self-deceived nor self-degraded and yet are poor. Many such are satisfied to remain poor. They are contented, industrious, and happy, and desire nothing else; but those among them who are dissatisfied, and are ambitious for better surroundings and greater scope should, and usually do, use their poverty as a spur to the exercise of their talents and energies. By self-improvement and attention to duty, they can rise into the fuller, more responsible life which they desire.

Devotion to duty is, indeed, not only the way out of that poverty which is regarded as restrictive, it is also the royal road to affluence, influence, and lasting joy, yea, even to perfection itself. When understood in its deepest sense it is seen to be related to all that is best and noblest in life. It includes energy, industry, concentrated attention to the business of one's life, singleness of purpose, courage and faithfulness, determination and self-reliance, and that self-abnegation which is the key to all real greatness. A singularly successful man was once asked, "What is the secret of your success?" and he replied, "Getting up at six o' clock in the morning, and minding my own business." Success, honour and influence always come to him who diligently attends to the business of his life, and religiously avoids interfering with the duties of others.

It may here be urged, and is usually so urged, that the majority of those who are in poverty - for instance, the mill and factory workers - have not the time or opportunity to give themselves to any special work. This is a mistake. Time and opportunity are always at hand, are with everybody at all times. Those of the poor above mentioned, who are content to remain where they are, can always be diligent in their factory labour, and sober and happy in their homes; but those of them who feel that they could better fill another sphere, can prepare for it by educating themselves in their spare time. The hard-worked poor are, above all, the people who need to economise their time and energies; and the youth who wishes to rise out of such poverty, must at the outset put aside the foolish and wasteful indulgences of alcohol, tobacco, sexual vice, late hours at music halls, clubs and gaming parties, and must give his evenings to the improvement of his mind in that course of education which is necessary to his advancement. By this method numbers of the most influential men throughout history - some of them among the greatest - have raised themselves from the commonest poverty; a fact which proves that the time of necessity is the hour of opportunity, and not as is so often imagined and declared, the destruction of opportunity; that the deeper the poverty, the greater is the incentive to action in those who are dissatisfied with themselves, and are bent upon achievement.

Poverty is an evil or it is not, according to the character and the condition of mind of the one that is in poverty. Wealth is an evil or not, in the same manner. Tolstoy chafed under his wealthy circumstances. To him they were a great evil. He longed for poverty as the covetous long for wealth. Vice, however, is always an evil, for it both degrades the individual who commits it, and is a menace to society. A logical and profound study of poverty will always bring us back to the individual, and to the human heart. When our social reformers condemn vice as they now condemn the rich; when they are as eager to abolish wrong-living as they now are to abolish low wages, we may look for a diminution in that form of degraded poverty which is one of the dark spots on our civilisation. Before such poverty disappears altogether, the human heart will have undergone, during the process of evolution, a radical change. When that heart is purged from covetousness and selfishness; when drunkenness, impurity, indolence and self-indulgence are driven for ever from the earth, then poverty and riches will be known no more, and every man will perform his duties with a joy so full and deep as is yet (except to the few whose hearts are already pure) unknown to men, and all will eat of the fruit of their labour in sublime self-respect and perfect peace.

6. Man's spiritual dominion

The kingdom over which man is destined to rule with undisputed sway is that of his own mind and life; but this kingdom, as already shown, is not separate from the universe, is not confined to itself alone; it is intimately related to entire humanity, to nature, to the current of events in which it is, for the time being, involved, and to the vast universe. Thus the mastery of this kingdom embraces the mastery of the kingdom embraces the mastery of the knowledge of life; it lifts a man into the supremacy of wisdom, bestowing upon him the gift of insight into human hearts, giving him the power to distinguish between good and evil, also to comprehend that which is above both good and evil, and to know the nature and consequences of deeds.

At present men are more or less under the sway of rebellious thoughts, and the conquest of these is the supreme conquest of life. The unwise think that everything can be mastered but oneself, and they seek for happiness for themselves and others by modifying external things. The transposing of outward effects cannot bring permanent happiness, or bestow wisdom; the patching and coddling of a sin-laden body cannot produce health and well-being. The wise know that there is no real mastery until self is subdued, that when oneself is conquered, the subjugation of externals is finally assured, and they find happiness for ever springing up within them, in the calm strength of divine virtue. They put away sin, and purify and strengthen the body by rising superior to the sway of its passions.

Man can reign over his own mind; can be lord over himself. Until he does so reign, his life is unsatisfactory and imperfect. His spiritual dominion is the empire of the mental forces of which his nature is composed. The body has no causative power. The ruling of the body - that is, of appetite and passion – is the discipline of mental forces. The subduing, modifying, redirecting and transmuting of the antagonising spiritual elements within, is the wonderful and mighty work which all men must, sooner or later, undertake. For a long time man regards himself as the slave of external forces, but there comes a day when his spiritual eyes open, and he sees that he has been a slave this long time to none and nothing but his own ungoverned, unpurified self. In that day, he rises up and, ascending his spiritual throne, he no longer obeys his desires, appetites, and passions, as their slave, but henceforth rules them as his subjects. The mental kingdom through which he has been wont to wander as a puling beggar and a whipped serf, he now discovers is his by right of lordly self control - his to set in order, to organise and harmonise, to abolish its dissensions and painful contradictions, and bring it to a state of peace.

Thus rising up and exercising his rightful spiritual authority, he enters the company of those kingly ones who in all ages have conquered and attained, who have overcome ignorance, darkness, and mental suffering, and have ascended into Truth.

7. Conquest: not resignation

He who has undertaken the sublime task of overcoming himself, does not resign himself to anything that is evil; he subjects himself only to that which is good. Resignation to evil is the lowest weakness; obedience to good is the highest power. To resign oneself to sin and sorrow, to ignorance and suffering, is to say in effect, "I give up; I am defeated; life is evil, and I submit."

Such resignation to evil is the reverse of religion. It is a direct denial of good; it elevates evil to the position of supreme power in the universe. Such submission to evil shows itself in a selfish and sorrowful life; a life alike devoid of strength against temptation, and of that joy and calm which are the manifestation of a mind that is dominated by good.

Man is not framed for perpetual resignation and sorrow, but for final victory and joy. All the spiritual laws of the universe are with the good man, for good preserves and shields. There are no laws of evil. Its nature is destruction and desolation.

The conscious modification of the character away from evil and towards good, forms, at present, no part in the common course of education. Even our religious teachers have lost this knowledge and practice, and cannot, therefore, instruct concerning it. Moral growth is, so far, in the great mass of mankind, unconscious, and is brought about by the stress and struggle of life. The time will come, however, when the conscious formation of character will form an important part in the education of youth, and when no man will be able to fill the position of preacher unless he be a man of habitual self-control, unblemished integrity, and exalted purity, so as to be able to give sound instruction in the making of character, which will then be the main feature of religion.

The doctrine herein set forth by the author is the doctrine of conquest over evil; the annihilation of sin; and necessarily the permanent establishment of man in the knowledge of good, and in the enjoyment of perpetual peace. This is the teaching of the Masters of religion in all ages. Howsoever it may have been disguised and distorted by the unenlightened, if is the doctrine of all the perfect ones that were, and will be the doctrine of all the perfect ones that are to come. It is the doctrine of Truth.

And the conquest is not of an evil without; not of evil men, or evil spirits, or evil things; but of the evil within; of evil thoughts, evil desires, evil deeds; for when every man has destroyed the evil within his own heart, to where in the whole vast universe will any one be able to point, and say, "There is evil?" In that great day when all men have become good within, all traces of evil will have vanished from the earth; sin and sorrow will be unknown; and there will be universal joy for evermore.

Foundation Stones To Happiness And Success

Editor's preface

This is one of the last MSS. written by James Allen. Like all his works it is eminently practical. He never wrote *theories,* or for the sake of writing, or to add another to his many books; but he wrote when he had a message, and it became a message *only when he had lived it out in his own life*, and knew that it was good. Thus he wrote *facts*, which he had proven by practice.

To live out the teaching of this book faithfully in every detail of life will lead one to more than happiness and success — even to Blessedness, Satisfaction and Peace.

LILY L. ALLEN
"Bryngoleu,"
Ilfracombe,
England.

Foreword

How does a man begin the building of a house? He first secures a plan of the proposed edifice, and then proceeds to build according to the plan, scrupulously following it in every detail, beginning with the foundation. Should he neglect the beginning - the beginning on a mathematical plan - his labour would be wasted, and his building, should it reach completion without tumbling to pieces, would be insecure and worthless. The same law holds good in any important work; the right beginning and first essential is *a definite mental plan on which to build.*

Nature will have no slipshod work, no slovenliness and she annihilates confusion, or rather, confusion is in itself annihilated. Order, definiteness, purpose, eternally prevail, and he who in his operations ignores these mathematical elements at once deprives himself of substantiality, completeness, happiness and success.

JAMES ALLEN

1. Right principles

It is wise to know what comes first, and what to do first. To begin anything in the middle or at the end is to make a muddle of it. The athlete who began by breaking the tape would not receive the prize. He must begin by facing the starter and toeing the mark, and even then a good start is important if he is to win. The pupil does not begin with algebra and literature, but with counting and ABC. So in life – the businessmen who begin at the bottom achieve the more enduring success; and the religious men who reach the highest heights of spiritual knowledge and wisdom are they who have stooped to serve a patient apprenticeship to the humbler tasks, and have not scorned the common experiences of humanity, or overlooked the lessons to be learned from them.

The first things in a sound life - and therefore, in a truly happy and successful life - are *right principles*. Without right principles to begin with, there will be wrong practices to follow with, and a bungled and wretched life to end with. All the infinite variety of calculations which tabulate the commerce and science of the world, come out of the ten figures; all the hundreds of thousands of books which constitute the literature of the world, and perpetuate its thought and genius, are built up from the twenty-six letters. The greatest astronomer cannot ignore the ten simple figures. The profoundest man of genius cannot dispense with the twenty-six simple characters. The fundamentals in all things are few and simple: yet without them there is no knowledge and no achievement. The fundamentals - the basic principles - in life, or true living, are also few and simple, and to learn them thoroughly, and study how to apply them to all the details of life, is to avoid confusion, and to secure a substantial foundation for the orderly building up of an invincible character and a permanent success; and to succeed in comprehending those principles in their innumerable ramifications in the labyrinth of conduct, is to become a Master of Life.

The first principles in life are principles of conduct. To name them is easy. As mere words they are on all men's lips, but as fixed sources of action, admitting of no compromise, few have learned them. In this short talk I will deal with five only of these principles. These five are among the simplest of the root principles of life, but they are those that come nearest to the everyday life, for they touch the artisan the businessman, the householder, the citizen at every point. Not one of them can be dispensed with but at severe cost, and he who perfects himself in their application will rise superior to many of the troubles and failures of life, and will come into these springs and currents of thought which flow harmoniously towards the regions of enduring success. The first of these principles is -

DUTY - A much-hackneyed word, I know, but it contains a rare jewel for him who will seek it by assiduous application. The principle of duty means strict adherence to one's own business, and just as strict non-interference in the business of others. The man who is continually instructing others, gratis, how to manage their affairs, is the one who most mismanages his own. Duty also means undivided attention to the matter in hand, intelligent concentration of the mind on the work to be done; it includes all that is meant by thoroughness, exactness, and efficiency. The details of duties differ with individuals, and each man should know his own duty better then he knows his neighbour's, and better than his neighbour knows his; but although the working details differ, the principle is always the same. Who has mastered the demands of duty?

HONESTY is the next principle. It means not cheating or overcharging another. It involves the absence of all trickery, lying, and deception by word, look, or gesture. It includes sincerity, the saying what you mean, and the meaning what you say. It scorns cringing policy and shining compliment. It builds up good reputations, and good reputations build up good businesses, and bright joy accompanies well-earned success. Who has scaled the heights of Honesty?

ECONOMY is the third principle. The conservation of one's financial resources is merely the vestibule leading towards the more spacious chambers of true economy. It means, as well, the husbanding of one's physical vitality and mental resources. It demands the conservation of energy by the avoidance of enervating self-indulgences and sensual habits. It holds for its follower strength, endurance, vigilance, and capacity to achieve. It bestows great power on him who learns it well. Who has realized the supreme strength of Economy?

LIBERALITY follows economy. It is not opposed to it. Only the man of economy can afford to be generous. The spendthrift, whether in money, vitality, or mental energy, wasted so much on his own miserable pleasures as to have none left to bestow upon others. The giving of money is the smallest part of liberality. There is a giving of thoughts, and deeds, and sympathy, the bestowing of goodwill, the being generous towards calumniators and opponents. It is a principle that begets a noble, far-reaching influence. It brings loving friends and staunch comrades, and is the foe of loneliness and despair. Who has measured the breadth of Liberality?

SELF–CONTROL is the last of these five principles, yet the most important. Its neglect is the cause of vast misery, innumerable failures, and tens of thousands of financial, physical, and mental wrecks. Show me the businessman who loses his temper with a customer over some trivial matter, and I will show you a man who, by that condition of mind, is doomed to failure. If all men practised even the initial stages of self-control, anger, with its consuming and destroying fire, would be unknown. The lessons of patience, purity, gentleness, kindness, and steadfastness, which are contained in the principle of self-control, are slowly learned by men, yet until they are truly learned a man's character and success are uncertain and insecure. Where is the man who has perfected himself in Self-Control? Where he may be, he is a master indeed.

The five principles are five practices, five avenues to achievement, and five sources of knowledge. It is an old saying and a good rule that "Practice makes perfect," and he who would make his own the wisdom which is inherent in those principles, must not merely have them on his lips, they must be established in his heart. To know them and receive what they alone can bring, he must *do* them, and give them out in his actions.

2. Sound methods

From the five foregoing Right Principles, when they are truly apprehended and practised, will issue *Sound Methods*. Right principles are manifested in harmonious action, and method is to life what law is to the universe. Everywhere in the universe there is the harmonious adjustment of parts, and it is this symmetry and harmony that reveals a cosmos, as distinguished from chaos. So in human life, the difference between a true life and a false, between one purposeful and effective and one purposeless and weak, is one of method. The false life is an incoherent jumble of thoughts, passions, and actions; the true life is an orderly adjustment of all its parts. It is all the difference between a mass of lumber and a smoothly working efficient machine. A piece of machinery in perfect working order is not only a useful, but an admirable and attractive thing; but when its parts are all out of gear, and refuse to be readjusted, its usefulness and attractiveness are gone, and it is thrown on the scrap-heap. Likewise a life perfectly adjusted in all its parts so as to achieve the highest point of efficiency, is not only a powerful, but an excellent and beautiful thing; whereas a life confused, inconsistent, discordant, is a deplorable exhibition of wasted energy.

If life is to be truly lived, method must enter into, and regulate, every detail of it, as it enters and regulates every detail of the wondrous universe of which we form a part. One of the distinguishing differences between a wise man and a foolish is, that the wise man pays careful attention to the smallest things, while the foolish man slurs over them, or neglects them altogether. Wisdom consists in maintaining things on their right relations, in keeping all things, the smallest as well as the greatest, in their proper places and times. To violate order is to produce confusion and discord, and *unhappiness* is but another name for discord.

The good businessman knows that system is three parts of success, and that disorder means failure. The wise man knows that disciplined, methodical living is three parts of happiness, and that looseness means misery. What is a fool but one who thinks carelessly, acts rashly, and lives loosely? What is a wise man but one who thinks carefully, acts calmly, and lives consistently?

The true method does not end with the orderly arrangement of the material things and external relations of life; this is but its beginning; it enters into the adjustment of the mind - the discipline of the passions, the elimination and choice of words in speech, the logical arrangement of the thoughts, and the selection of right actions.

To achieve a life rendered sound, successful, and sweet by the pursuance of sound methods, one must begin, not by neglect of the little everyday things, but by assiduous attention to them. Thus the hour of rising is important, and its regularity significant; as also are the timing of retiring to rest, and the number of hours given to sleep. Between the regularity and irregularity of meals, and the care and carelessness with which they are eaten, is all the difference between a good and bad digestion (with all that this applies) and an irritable or comfortable frame of mind, with its train of good or bad consequences, for, attaching to these meal-times and meal-ways are matters of both physiological and psychological significance. The due division of hours for business and for play, not confusing the two, the orderly fitting in of all the details of one's business, times for solitude, for silent thought and for effective action, for eating and for abstinence - all these things must have their lawful place in the life of him whose "daily round" is to proceed with the minimum degree of friction, who is to get the most of usefulness, influence, and joy out of life.

But all this is but the beginning of that comprehensive method which embraces the whole life and being. When this smooth order and logical consistency is extended to the words and actions, to the thoughts and desires, then wisdom emerges from folly, and out of weakness comes power sublime. When a man so orders his mind as to produce a beautiful working harmony between all its parts, then he reaches the highest wisdom, the highest efficiency, the highest happiness.

But this is the end; and he who would reach the end must begin at the beginning. He must systematise and render logical and smooth the smallest details of his life, proceeding step by step towards the finished accomplishment. But each step will yield its own particular measure of strength and gladness.

To sum up, method produces that smoothness which goes with strength and efficiency. Discipline is method applied to the mind. It produces that calmness which goes with power and happiness. Method is *working* by rule; discipline is *living* by rule. But working and living are not separate; they are but two aspects of character, of life.

Therefore, be orderly in work; be accurate in speech, be logical in thought. Between these and slovenliness, inaccuracy and confusion, is the difference between success and failure, music and discord, happiness and misery.

The adoption of sound methods of working, acting, thinking – in a word, of *living,* is the surest and safest foundation for sound health, sound success, sound peace of mind. The foundation of unsound methods will be found to be unstable, and to yield fear and unrest even while it appears to succeed, and when its time of failure comes, it is grievous indeed.

3. True actions

Following on Right Principles and Methods come True Actions. One who is striving to grasp true principles and work with sound methods will soon come to perceive that details of conduct cannot be overlooked - that, indeed, those details are fundamentally distinctive or creative, according to their nature, and are, therefore, of deep significance and comprehensive importance; and this perception and knowledge of the nature and power of passing actions will gradually open and grow within him as an added vision, a new revelation. As he acquires this insight his progress will be more rapid, his pathway in life more sure, his days more serene and peaceful; in all things he will go the true and direct way, unswayed and untroubled by the external forces that play around and about him. Not that he will be indifferent to the welfare and happiness of those about him; that is quite another thing; but he will be indifferent to their opinions, to their ignorance, to their ungoverned passions. By *True Actions,* indeed, is meant acting rightly towards others, and the right-doer knows that actions in accordance with truth are but for the happiness of those about him, and he will do them even though an occasion may arise when some one near to him may advise or implore him to do otherwise.

True actions may easily be distinguished from false by all who wish so to distinguish in order that they may avoid false action, and adopt true. As in the material world we distinguish things by their form, colour, size, etc., choosing those things which we require, and putting by those things which are not useful to us, so in the spiritual world of deeds, we can distinguish between those that are bad and those that are good by their nature, their aim, and their effect and can choose and adopt those that are good, and ignore those that are bad.

In all forms of progress, *avoidance of the bad* always precedes *acceptance and knowledge of the good,* just as a child at school learns to do its lessons right by having repeatedly pointed out to it how it has done them wrong. If one does not know what is wrong and how to avoid it, how can he know what is right and how to practise it? Bad, or untrue, actions are those that spring from a consideration of one's own happiness only, and ignore the happiness of others, that arise in violent disturbances of the mind and unlawful desires, or that call for concealment in order to avoid undesirable complications. Good or true actions are those that spring from a consideration for others, that arise in calm reason and harmonious thought framed on moral principles or that will not involve the doer in shameful consequences if brought into the full light of day.

The right-doer will avoid those acts of personal pleasure and gratification which by their nature bring annoyance, pain, or suffering to others, no matter how insignificant those actions may appear to be. He will begin by putting away these; he will gain a knowledge of the unselfish and true by first sacrificing the selfish and untrue. He will learn not to speak or act in anger, or envy, or resentment, but will study how to control his mind, and will restore it to calmness before acting; and, most important of all, he will avoid, as he would the drinking of deadly poison, those acts of trickery, deceit, double-dealing, in order to gain some personal profit of advantage, and which lead, sooner or later, to exposure and shame for the doer of them. If a man is prompted to do a thing which he needs to conceal, and which he would not lawfully and frankly defend if it were examined of witness, he should know by that that it is a wrong act and therefore to be abandoned without a further moment's consideration.

The carrying out of this principle of honesty and sincerity of action, too, will further lead him into such a path of thoughtfulness in right-doing as will enable him to avoid doing those things which would involve him in the deceptive practices of other people. Before signing papers, or entering into verbal or written arrangements, or engaging himself to others in any way at their request, particularly if they be strangers, he will first inquire into the nature of the work or undertaking, and so, enlightened, he will know exactly what to do, and will be fully aware of the import of his action. To the right-doer *thoughtlessness* is a crime. Thousands of actions done with good intent lead to disastrous consequences because they are acts of thoughtlessness, and it is well said "that the way to hell is paved with good intentions." The man of true actions is, above all things, thoughtful:- "Be ye therefore wise as serpents and harmless as doves."

The term *Thoughtlessness* covers a wide field in the realm of deeds. It is only by increasing in thoughtfulness that a man can come to understand the nature of actions, and can, thereby, acquire the power of *always doing that which is right*. It is impossible for a man to be thoughtful and act foolishly. Thoughtfulness embraces wisdom.

It is not enough that an action is prompted by a good impulse or intention; it must arise in *thoughtful consideration* if it is to be a true action; and the man who wishes to be permanently happy in himself and a power for good to others must concern himself only with true actions. "I did it with the best of intentions," is a poor excuse from one who has thoughtlessly involved himself in the wrong-doing of others. His bitter experience should teach him to act more thoughtfully in the future.

True actions can only spring from a true mind, and therefore while a man is learning to distinguish and choose between the false and the true, he is correcting and perfecting his mind, and is thereby rendering it more harmonious and felicitous, more efficient and powerful. As he acquires the "inner eye" to clearly distinguish the right in all the details of life, and the faith and knowledge to do it, he will realise that he is building the house of his character and life upon a rock which the winds of failure and the storms of persecution can never undermine.

4. True speech

Truth is known by practice only. Without sincerity there can be no knowledge of Truth; and true speech is the beginning of all sincerity. Truth in all its native beauty and original simplicity consists in abandoning and not doing all those things which are untrue, and in embracing and doing all those things which are true. True speech is therefore one of the elementary beginnings in the life of Truth. Falsehood, and all forms of deception; slander and all forms of evil-speaking - these must be totally abandoned and abolished before the mind can receive even a small degree of spiritual enlightenment. The liar and slanderer is lost in darkness; so deep is his darkness that he cannot distinguish between good and evil, and he persuades himself that his lying and evil-speaking are necessary and good, that he is thereby protecting himself and other people.

Let the would-be student of "higher things" look to himself and beware of self-delusion. If he is given to uttering words that deceive, or to speaking evil of others – if he speaks in insincerity, envy, or malice - then he has not yet begun to study higher things. He may be studying metaphysics, or miracles, or psychic phenomena, or astral wonders – he may be studying how to commune with invisible beings, to travel invisibly during sleep, or to produce curious phenomena - he may even study spirituality theoretically and as a mere book study, but if he is a deceiver and a backbiter, the higher life is hidden from him. For the higher things are these – *uprightness, sincerity, innocence, purity, kindness, gentleness, faithfulness, humility, patience, pity, sympathy, self-sacrifice, joy, goodwill, love* – and he who would study them, know them, and make them his own, must *practice* them, there is no other way.

Lying and evil-speaking belong to the lowest forms of spiritual ignorance, and there can be no such thing as spiritual enlightenment while they are practised. Their parents are selfishness and hatred.

Slander is akin to lying, but it is even more subtle, as it is frequently associated with indignation, and by assuming more successfully the appearance of truth, it ensnares many who would not tell a deliberate falsehood. For there are two sides to slander - there is *the making of repeating of it,* and there is *the listening to it and acting upon it.* The slanderer would be powerless without a listener. Evil words require an ear that is receptive to evil in which they may fall, before they can flourish; therefore he who listens to a slanderer, who believes it, and allows himself to be influenced against the person whose character and reputation are defamed, is in the same position as the one who framed or repeated the evil report. The evil-speaker is a positive slanderer; the evil-listener is a passive slanderer. The two are co-operators in the propagation of evil.

Slander is a common vice and a dark and deadly one. An evil report begins in ignorance, and pursues its blind way in darkness. It generally takes its rise in a misunderstanding. Some one feels that he or she has been badly treated, and, filled with indignation and resentment, unburdens himself to his friends and others in vehement language, exaggerating the enormity of the supposed offence on account of the feeling of injury by which he is possessed; he is listened to and sympathised with; the listeners, without hearing *the other person's* version of what has taken place, and on no other proof than the violent words of an angry man or woman, become cold in their attitude towards the one spoken against, and repeat to others what they have been told, and as such repetition is always more or less inaccurate, a distorted and altogether untrue report is soon passing from mouth to mouth.

It is because slander is such a common vice that it can work the suffering and injury that it does. It is because so many (not deliberate wrong-doers, and unconscious of the nature of the evil into which they so easily fall) are ready to allow themselves to be influenced against one whom they have hitherto regarded as honourable, that an evil report can do its deadly work. Yet its work is only amongst those who have not altogether acquired the virtue of true speech, the cause of which is a truth-loving mind. When one who has not entirely freed himself from repeating or believing an evil report about another, hears of an evil report about himself, his mind becomes aflame with burning resentment, his sleep is broken and his peace of mind is destroyed. He thinks the cause of all his suffering is in the other man and what that man has said about him, and is ignorant of the truth that *the root and cause of his suffering lies in his own readiness to believe an evil report about another.* The virtuous man - he who has attained to true speech, and whose mind is sealed against even the appearance of evil-speaking - cannot be injured and disturbed about any evil reports concerning himself; and although his reputation may for a time be stained *in the minds of those who are prone to suggestions of evil,* his integrity remains untouched and his character unsoiled; for no one can be stained by the evil deeds of another, but only by his own wrongdoing. And so, through all misrepresentation, misunderstanding, and contumely, he is untroubled and unrevengeful; his sleep is undisturbed, and his mind remains in peace.

True speech is the beginning of a pure, wise and well-ordered life. If one would attain to purity of life, if he would lessen the evil and suffering of the world, let him abandon falsehood and slander in thought and word, let him avoid even the appearance of these things, for there are no lies and slanders so deadly as those which are half-truths, and let him not be a participant in evil-speaking by listening to it. Let him also have compassion on the evil-speaker, knowing how such a one is binding himself to suffering and unrest; for no liar can know the bliss of Truth; no slanderer can enter the kingdom of peace.

By the words which he utters is a man's spiritual condition declared; by these also is he finally and infallibly adjudged, for as the Divine Master of the Christian world has declared, "By thy words shalt thou be justified, and by thy words shalt thou be condemned.

5. Equal-mindedness

To be equally-minded is to be peacefully-minded, for a man cannot be said to have arrived at peace who allows his mind to be disturbed and thrown off the balance by occurrences.

The man of wisdom is dispassionate, and meets all things with the calmness of a mind in repose and free from prejudice. He is not a partisan, having put away passion, and he is always at peace with himself and the world, not taking sides nor defending himself, but sympathising with all.

The partisan is so convinced that his own opinion and his own side is right, and all that goes contrary to them is wrong, that he cannot think there is any good in the other opinion and the other side. He lives in a continual fever of attack and defence, and has no knowledge of the quiet peace of an equal mind.

The equal-minded man watches himself in order to check and overcome even the appearance of passion and prejudice in his mind, and by so doing he develops sympathy for others, and comes to understand their position and particular state of mind; and as he comes to understand others, he perceives the folly of condemning them and opposing himself to them. Thus there grows up in his heart a divine charity which cannot be limited, but which is extended to all things that live and strive and suffer.

When a man is under the sway of passion and prejudice he is spiritually blind. Seeing nothing but good in his own side, and nothing but evil in the other, he cannot see anything as it really is, not even his own side; and not understanding himself, he cannot understand the hearts of others, and thinks it is right that he should condemn them. Thus there grows up in his heart a dark hatred for those who refuse to see with him and who condemn him in return, he becomes separated from his fellow-men, and confines himself to a narrow torture chamber of his own making.

Sweet and peaceful are the days of the equal-minded man, fruitful in good, and rich in manifold blessings. Guided by wisdom, he avoids those pathways which lead down to hatred and sorrow and pain, and takes those which lead up to love and peace and bliss. The occurrences of life do not trouble him, nor does he grieve over those things which are regarded by mankind as grievous, but which must befall all men in the ordinary course of nature. He is neither elated by success nor cast down by failure. He sees the events of his life arrayed in their proper proportions, and can find no room for selfish wishes or vain regrets, for vain anticipations and childish disappointments.

And how is this equal-mindedness - this blessed state of mind and life - acquired? Only by overcoming one's self, only by purifying one's own heart, for the purification of the heart leads to unbiased comprehension, unbiased comprehension leads to equal-mindedness, and equal-mindedness leads to peace. The impure man is swept helplessly away on the waves of passion; the pure man guides himself into the harbour of rest. The fool says, "I have an opinion;" the wise man goes about his business.

6. Good results

A considerable portion of the happenings of life comes to us without any *direct* choosing on our part, and such happenings are generally regarded as having no relation to our will or character, but as appearing fortuitously; as occurring without a cause. Thus one is spoken of as being "lucky," and another "unlucky," the inference being that each has received something which he never earned, never caused. Deeper thought, and a clearer insight into life convinces us, however, that nothing happens without a cause, and that cause and effect are always related in perfect adjustment and harmony. This being so, every happening directly affecting us is intimately related to our own will and character, is, indeed, an effect justly related to a cause having its seat in our consciousness. In a word, involuntary happenings of life are the results of our own thoughts and deeds. This, I admit, is not apparent on the surface; but what fundamental law, even in the physical universe, *is* so apparent? If thought, investigation, and experiment are necessary to the discovery of the principles which relate one material atom to another, even so are they imperative to the perception and understanding of the mode of action which relate one mental condition to another; and such modes, such laws, are known by the right-doer, by him who has acquired an understanding mind by the practice of true actions.

We reap as we sow. Those things which come to us, though not by our own *choosing,* are by our *causing.* The drunkard did not choose the delirium tremens or insanity which overtook him, but he caused it by his own deeds. In this case the law is plain to all minds, but where it is not so plain, it is nonetheless true. Within ourselves is the deep-seated cause of all our sufferings, the spring of all our joys. Alter the inner world of thoughts, and the other world of events will cease to bring you sorrow; make the heart pure, and to you all things will be pure, all occurrences happy and in true order.

> *"Within yourselves deliverance must be sought,*
> *Each man his prison makes.*
> *Each hath such lordship as the loftiest ones;*
> *Nay, for with Powers above, around, below,*
> *As with all flesh and whatsoever lives,*
> *Act maketh joy or woe."*

Our life is good or bad, enslaved or free, according to its causation in our thoughts, for out of these thoughts spring all our deeds, and from these deeds come equitable results. We cannot seize good results violently, like a thief, and claim and enjoy them, but we can bring them to pass by setting in motion the causes within ourselves.

Men strive for money, sigh for happiness, and would gladly possess wisdom, yet fail to secure these things, while they see others to whom these blessings appear to come unbidden. The reason is that they have generated causes which prevent the fulfilment of their wishes and efforts.

Each life is a perfectly woven network of causes and effects, of efforts (or lack of efforts) and results, and good results can only be reached by initiating good efforts, good causes. The doer of true actions, who pursues sound methods, grounded on right principles will not need to strive and struggle for good results; they will be there as the effects of his righteous rule of life. He will reap the fruit of his own actions and the reaping will be in gladness and peace.

This truth of sowing and reaping in the moral sphere is a simple one, yet men are slow to understand and accept it. We have been told by a Wise One that "the children of darkness are wiser in their day than the children of light", and who would expect, in the material world, to reap and eat where he had not sown and planted? Or who would expect to reap wheat in the field where he had sown tares, and would fall to weeping and complaining if he did not? Yet this is just what men do in the spiritual field of mind and deed. They do evil, and expect to get from it good, and when the bitter harvesting comes in all its ripened fullness, they fall into despair, and bemoan the hardness and injustice of their lot, usually attributing it to the evil deeds of others, refusing even to admit the possibility of its cause being hidden in themselves, in their own thoughts and deeds. The children of light - those who are searching for the fundamental principles of right living, with a view to making themselves into wise and happy beings – must train themselves to observe this law of cause and effect in thought, word and deed, as implicitly and obediently as the gardener obeys the law of sowing and reaping. He does not even question the law; he recognises and obeys it. When the wisdom which he instinctively practices in his garden, is practiced by men in the garden of their minds – when the law of the sowing of deeds is so fully recognised that it can no longer be doubted or questioned – then it will be just as faithfully followed by the sowing of those actions which will bring about a reaping of happiness and well-being for all. As the children of matter obey the laws of matter, so let the children of spirit obey the laws of spirit, for the law of matter and the law of spirit are one; they are but two aspects of one thing; the out-working of one principle in opposite directions.

If we observe right principles, or causes, wrong effects cannot possibly accrue. If we pursue sound methods, no shoddy thread can find its way into the web of our life, no rotten brick enter into the building of our character to render it insecure; and if we do true actions, what but good results can come to pass; for to say that good causes can produce bad effects is to say that nettles can be reaped from a sowing of corn.

He who orders his life along the moral lines thus briefly enunciated, will attain to such a state of insight and equilibrium as to render him permanently happy and perennially glad; all his efforts will be seasonally planted; all the issues of his life will be good, and though he may not become a millionaire as indeed he will have no desire to become such - he will acquire the gift of peace, and true success will wait upon him as its commanding master.

Men And Systems

Introduction

THE unceasing change, the insecurity, and the misery of life make it necessary to find some basis of certainty on which to rest if happiness and peace of mind are to be maintained. All science, philosophy, and religion are some many efforts in search of this permanent basis; all interpretations on the universe, whether from the material or spiritual side, are so many attempts to formulate some unifying principle or principles by which to reconcile the fluctuations and contradictions of life.

it has been said that mathematics is the only exact science; that is, the only science that eternally works out true without a single exception. Yet mathematics is but the body of which ethics is the spirit. There is not a mathematical problem but has its ethical counterpart, and the spirit of ethics is as eternally exact as the form of mathematics.

It is being discovered that all natural sciences are fundamentally mathematical. Even music popularly considered to be as far removed from mathematics as possible-is now known to be strictly mathematical. The science of harmony revealed certain fixed tones which never vary in their relative proportions, and all of which can be numerically resolved. These tones, like the numbers which represent them, are eternally fixed; and though their combinations- also like the combinations of numbers- are infinite, a given combination will always produce the same result.

This mathematical foundation in all things is the keystone in the temple of science; and this mathematical certainty constitutes the "rock of ages," and the "great peace," on which and in which the saints and sages have ever found rest from the stress and turmoil of life.

Human life and evolution at present is the learning of those preliminary lessons which are leading the race towards the mastery and understanding of this basic or divine knowledge; for without such a permanent, exact mathematical basis no lesson could be learnt. When human beings are spoken of as learning the lessons of God or of life, two things are inferred, namely; (1) A state of ignorance on the part of the learner, and (2) that there is some definite knowledge which he has to acquire. This is seen plainly in a child at school. Its lessons imply that there is a permanent principle of knowledge towards which it is progressing. Without such knowledge there could be no lessons.

Thus, when one speaks of erring men as learning the lessons of life, he infers, whether he realizes it or not, the existence of a permanent basis of knowledge towards the possession of which all men are moving.

This basic principle, a knowledge of which the whole race will ultimately acquire, is best represented by the term Divine Justice. Human justice differs with every man according to this own light or darkness, but there can be no variation in that Divine Justice by which the universe is eternally sustained. Divine Justice is spiritual mathematics. As with figures and objects, whether simple or complex, there is a right and unvarying result, and no amount of ignorance or deliberate falsification can ever make it otherwise, so with every combination of thoughts or deeds, whether good or bad, there is an unvarying and inevitable consequence which nothing can avert.

If this were not so, if we could have effect without cause, or consequence unrelated to act, experience could never lead to knowledge, there would be no foundation of security, and no lessons could be learnt.

Thus every effect has a cause, and cause and effect are in such intimate relationship as to leave no room for injustice to creep in. Nevertheless, there is ignorance, and, through ignorance, the doing of life's lessons wrongly; and this doing of life's sums wrongly is that error, or sin, which is the source of man's sufferings. How often the child at school weeps because it cannot do its sums correctly! And older children in the school of life do the same thing when the sum of their actions has worked out in the form of suffering instead of happiness.

The ground of certainty, then, on which we can securely rest amid all the incidents of life is the mathematical exactitude of the moral law. The moral order of the universe is not, cannot, be disproportionate, for if it were the universe would fall to pieces. If a brick house cannot stand unless it be built in accordance with certain geometrical proportions, how could a vast universe, with all its infinite complexities of form and motion, proceed in unbroken majesty from age to age unless guided by unerring and infallible justice?

All the physical laws with which men are acquainted never vary in their operations. Given the same cause, there will always be the same effect. All the spiritual laws with which men are acquainted have, and must have, the same infallibility in their operations. Given the same thought or deed in a life circumstance, and the result will always be the same. Without this fundamental ethical justice there could be no human society, for its is the just reactions of the deeds of individuals which prevents society from tottering to its fall.

It thus follows that the inequalities of life, as regards the distribution of happiness and suffering, are the outworking of moral forces operating along lines of flawless accuracy, this perfect law, is the one great fundamental certainty in life, the finding of which ensures a man's perfection, makes him wise and enlightened, and fills him with rejoicing and peace.

Take away a belief in this certainty from a man's consciousness, and he is adrift on a self created ocean of chance, without rudder, chart, or compass. He has no ground on which to build a character or life, no incentive for noble deeds, no center for moral action; he has no island of peace and no harbor of refuge. Even the crudest idea of God as of a great man whose mind is perfect, who cannot err, and who has "no, variables nor shadow of turning," is a popular expression of a belief in this basic principle of Divine Justice.

According to this principle there is neither favor nor change, but unerring and unchangeable right. Thus all the sufferings of men are right as effects, their causes being the mistakes of ignorance; but as effects they will pass away. Man cannot suffer for something which he has never done, or never left undone for this would be an effect without a cause.

Man suffers through and himself. Where the effect is there is the cause. Its seat is within, not without. The things which men are reaping to-day are of the same kind which they formerly sowed. The good man of to-day may be reaping the results of past evil; the bad man of to-day may be reaping the results of past good. Seen thus, this divine principle throws an illuminating light on those cases (common enough) where the good suffer and fail, and the bad enjoy and prosper. Things as they are did not spring into existence without a cause. They have behind them a long train of causes and effects, and another such train will follow them in the future. In viewing the objects in a landscape we allow for perspective; we must do the same in viewing events.

This principle of Divine Justice is not distinct from Divine Law. It is the same. Partial men separate justice from love, and even regard them as antagonistic, but in the divine life they blend into one.

Nothing can transcend right. Nothing can be more loving than that we should experience the sequences of ignorance and error, and so become "perfected through suffering." In this Divine Love, which never alters, never errs, never passes over a single deed, we have a sure rock of salvation, for that which could shift and change could afford no foothold. Only in the unchangeable, the eternally true, is there permanent peace and safety. Resorting to this divine principle, abandoning all evil, and cling to good, we come to a knowledge and realization of that basis of certainty on which we can firmly stand through all life's changes; we have found the rock of ages and the refuge of the saints.

JAMES ALLEN
"BRYNGOLEU,"
ILFRACOMBE.

1. Men and systems
Their correlations and combined results

THERE is to-day a widespread revolt against those modes of human activity designated "Systems," and these systems are almost invariably referred to as something distinct from, and yet directing, controlling, or tyrannizing over, humanity itself. Thus the leaders in the revolt referred to speak of the "commercial system", the "social system", the "competitive system," the "political system," and so on; and the particular system condemned is made responsible for-made the cause of -certain widespread evils, such as poverty, vice, &c., as though "systems" were some sort of discarnate and gigantic despots, enslaving and crushing an innocent and unwilling humanity.

Such an arbitrary and external form of system has no existence; it is a delusion. Human systems cannot be separated from human desires and needs; they are, indeed, the visible outworking of those desires and needs. A system is none other than the combined and concerted mode of action of the community; it signifies a tacit agreement on the part of all, or nearly all, that things should be so and so; it is a method in which human kind agree to act. And as men act, so systems appear; as they cease to act, so they disappear.

And let it be understood that such agreement to act has no reference to, or bearing upon, a man's attitude towards a system- whether for or against- but depends upon his actions. A man may violently condemn a system with his lips, yet show that he is in agreement with it in his heart by the fact that he continues to act in accordance with it, to follow it out in his daily life. We are all aware of that form of religious hypocrisy (nearly always unconscious) that continues to commit the sin which it violently denounces; thus showing, in practice, a fundamental agreement with that which, superficially and ion theory, is opposed. And this form of unconscious inconsistency is not confined to religion; it is a pronounced factor in all moral activities, and is nowhere more strongly in evidence than in those directions where the reform of "existing systems" is, theoretically at any rate, the primary aim. Thus, when i have asked some socialists, who condemn the present capitalist system as a system of getting rich on the labor of the poor, why they themselves life on dividends- that is, on the fruits of other men's labor, thus propagating every day that which they denounce as an evil-the reply almost invariably has been, "You should blame the system, not me." This reply shows that such people regard themselves as the helpless victims of a tyrannical something which exists external to, and independent of , themselves and their actions, and which they call a "system." But a little reflection will show that which they denounce as the "system" is none other than the viewing as evil certain actions in others which they regard as good in themselves.

Human systems are human modes of action which are dependent for their continuance on a fundamental tacit agreement among men to continue to act in the same way; and such agreement implies that those who continue to enact any particular system must be prepared to meet and to accept its disadvantages as well as its advantages; for in the struggle for advantage there must always be the corresponding disadvantage; in the battle of human interests there must always be both victory and defeat.

Viewed in this light, the term "innocent victims of the system," so much in vogue, is seen to be shallow and delusive. There are no innocent victims of a system in which all engage either in the letter or the spirit; if guilt there be, then all are guilty, and the innocence is superficial and apparent, not fundamental and real. In reality, however, there is neither innocence nor guild attached to a human system which has evolved through long processes of struggle and time. There is merely the victory and happiness on the one hand, and the defeat and misery on the other; and the defeated are not the innocent, nor the victorious the guilty, for both these conditions in social life are the just effects of men's actions, as victory and defeat attach to a battle or a race.

To make this more plain, let us take a simple illustration. Here are ten men who mutually agree to engage, among themselves, in certain forms of gambling. Now, the object of each of these men is to win, and so increase his wealth, yet they all know that there is also the possibility of losing; know, indeed, that some must lose, for such is the unavoidable hazard of the game. Immediately these men commence to act, by laying down their stakes, they have created a system which might be called "the gambling system," and the advantages and disadvantages of such a system soon become apparent. There is ceaseless fluctuation of their combined wealth-some winning and becoming rich, and then again losing and becoming poor; but ultimately some lose all they possess and have to retire defeated, while others acquire the losers' part and become rich on their gains.

Now, it cannot be said of the winners that they are guilty of exploiting and crushing down the losers; nor can it be said of the losers that they are the innocent victims of the system of gambling in which they are engaged. In the mental attitude and actions of these ten men there is neither innocence nor guilt, but a mutual engagement in a method, with its inevitable results, namely, the reaping of its advantages on the one hand, the suffering from its disadvantages on the other.

In like manner, of the various systems in which men have involved themselves, there are no innocent victims, no guilty tyrants. Victims there are, if men choose to apply that term to the defeated, or to those who, for the time being, are suffering loss; but they are the victims of their own deeds, and not of an overruling and compelling injustice outside themselves. Of the ten men who engage in gambling, none are victimized, none can possibly be victimized, but themselves. Those outside the system- that is, those who do not encourage and propagate it by their acts- remain untouched, uninjured by it. So if our present commercial system should be a "system of greed," as many social reformers style it, then not by any possibility whatever could any but the greedy be injured by it.

Doubtless there is much greed in the world, for in its present stage of evolution humanity is learning its lessons largely along selfish paths; but greed can never have any existence in external "system," it can only exist in human hearts; nor can greed injure any but the greedy. Commercialism is free from greed in the hands of those who have destroyed greed in themselves. But they who are greedily will taint everything-even religion-with their own impure condition.

Industrialism, the outworking of a nation's energies and abilities, is wholesome and noble; it is covetousness which produces woe, and the sole sufferers from covetousness are the covetous themselves.

I will here anticipate the common query, "What of the innocent victims of the rapacious company promoter?" by replying (and this reply will be found adaptable to all human conditions and systems) they are not innocent, but have the same attitude of mind as the unscrupulous company promoter, namely, the desire to obtain money, and as much of its as possible, without laboring for it. The company promoter is the instrument through whom they reap the results of their own greed, and fall victims to their own covetousness.

Social reformers may denounce the system of "capitalism" or "commercialism", but so long as they themselves continue to enact that side of commercialism which is most akin to covetousness, namely, its speculative as distinguished from its industrial side, by keeping a keen eye to "good investments," and following up increased "dividends" with avidity, just so ling will that which they call "a system of greed" (and indeed to them it is such) continue.

Those who are striving to life by speculation, on the fruits of another's labors or who have the spirit to do should the opportunity arise (and the number of those who are anxious to acquire money without giving its equivalent is very large), should not bemoan the existence of want and poverty, but should perceive and receive such conditions as the inevitable disadvantages of the method which they are acting out, as luxury and riches are its advantages.

The hope of one day becoming suddenly rich without working for it, and living ever after a life of unbroken ease, is a common chimera among the poor. While covetousness continues to sway the human mind, want and poverty will continue.

Men desire, and then they act, and they combined acts constitute what men call "systems". The ten gamblers desired to increase their wealth without laboring for it, and at each other's loss, and they acted accordingly. Their combined actions constituted the system with its combination of results. Systems are, therefore, deeds- combined and reciprocal of a number of individuals; and the so-called evils in the world which men attribute to systems as distinguished from men are the reactions upon individuals of their own deeds.

A system cannot be "unjust," because men inevitably reap the just effects of their own deeds. The evils which prevail in the world are indications of justice, not injustice. Poverty and want are the natural disadvantages of the present social life, or system- that is, of the way in which men agree to act. There is suffering, but there is not injustice. It could not be said of those among the ten gamblers who were reduced to poverty that they were treated unjustly by the winners, or that they were the innocent victims of the system of gambling. Their lot was just; their poverty being the, inevitable result of their own actions.

Recently a socialist friend of mine was somewhat violently condemning landlords and landlords, and i pulled him up by saying," But why do you condemn landlords, seeing that you are one yourself? Have you not, only a few weeks ago, added another piece of land to that which you already possessed?" He replied, "It's the system, not me. So long as the present system lasts I shall have to work with it; but when it is altered, i shall be willing to give up my land."

If a gambler of were continually condemning the "system" of gambling as a bad one, and yet continued to gamble, we should justly say that he was confused both in his morals and perceptions; and he is equally confused who, while condemning any other system, social, political, or whatsoever, yet continues to act it out. Such a man does not, in his heart, regard the system as bad, but as good and just; this is evidenced by the fact that he continues to propagate it by his actions.

Systems are to men as light to the sun, rain to the clouds, or thoughts to the mind. They are both men and the deeds of men. To regard them as separate from men is confusion of thought and principle. Nor can there possibly be any injustice in their outworking, for the reaction of ignorant deeds is certain; the recompense of enlightened deeds is sure.

I see no evil in systems; i see evil in ignorance and wrong-doing. All systems are legitimate, for men have liberty to act in their own way. The ten gamblers who mutually agree to enrich and impoverish each other have nobody to blame but themselves; and if the winners are satisfied with their gains, the losers should be equally satisfied with their losses; if they are not, then they should look to themselves and remedy their deeds. Their poverty is good discipline, in that it is driving them to seek a better way of action.

If a man regards a system as bad, he should withdraw from it in practice, and should bend his actions in another direction; for immediately two men act in concert a system is formed, and the good and the bad which lurk in their actions will soon be manifested in the system which they have launched forth.

In the life of humanity, in systems, in what are called good and bad, are visible the outworking of the combined results of men's deeds; and in all, through all, and over all, justice reigns eternally triumphant.

2. Work, wages, and well-being

ACTIVITY is a necessity of existence, and usefulness is the object of being. Nature at once cuts off that which has become useless. Her economy is faultless, and she will not be burdened with things which have ceased to be of service in her progressive workshop. Nor does she allow her handy tools to lie unused, nor her bright things to rust. Where so ever there is ability, there also are scope and opportunity; where there is energy, there also are legitimate channels for its exercise; where there is a soaring mind, the means of achievement are ready to hand. As the field waits for the plough, the sea for the ship-, and the port for produce, so Nature in all her departments, whether material or mental, stands ready to co-operate with man in all his labors, and to reward him according to his diligence and industry. The statement, "There is no scope for my abilities," is either an expression of vanity, an excuse for negligence, or a confession of lack of resource, or of inability to utilize opportunity. Ability need never lie unused for a moment. There is unlimited scope for all abilities. All that is required is the capacity for work.

Of all abilities, the capacity for work is the most useful and necessary, and its possession is a glorious power; and this men discover when they are disabled, or stricken down with sickness. When they are thus forcibly prevented from engaging in wholesome, invigorating labor, what would they not give to have once again the spirited and glowing use of brain or muscle, or to spend exuberant strength in healthful exertion?

Work is of two kinds- it is either loving labor or enforced slavery. The man whose sole object is to get through his work in order to draw his pay, who has no love for, and no interest in his work, beyond what it represents in cash, is a slave and not a true worker. He labors only under the compulsion of necessity. His entire interest is in getting instead of in doing. He gives his labor irksomely and perfunctorily, but receives his pay with eagerness, striving, when he things he safely can, to give less and less labor, and get more and more wages. "Less work and more pay," is the cry of slaves, and not of men.

On the contrary, the man whose heart is centered in his work, who aims at the perfect performance of his duty, is a true worker whose usefulness and influence are cumulative and progressive, carrying him on from success to greater and greater success, from low spheres of labor to higher and higher still. Thinking little or nothing of the wages, and much of reward, but eager and willing in service, he is sealed by Nature as one of her chosen sons, fitted by virtue of his unselfish labors to receive the greater excellence and fuller reward.

For while full recompense may, and frequently does, escape the man who covetously seeks it, it cannot be withheld from him who ignores it in his work. For the true recompense is never withheld, but in the selfish desire to secure the recompense without giving its equivalent, disappointment is the pay received, and the expected reward does not appear.

The wages of work are sure. In the universal economy no man is cheated; he cannot be defrauded of his just earnings, for every effort receives its proportionate result; first work as the cause, and then wages as the effect. But while wages is the result, it is not the end; it is only a means to a still greater and more far-reaching result and end, namely, the progress and increased happiness both of the individual and the race-in word, to wellbeing.

The receiving of so much money for work done does not represent wages in its entirety; it is, indeed, only a small portion of the actual wages of true work; while the man who considers that the end of work is reached when he has received the money due receives all he bargains for, he does not derive complete satisfaction from his labors, nor comprehend or enter the higher spheres of knowledge and usefulness which are reserved for the devotes of unselfish duty.

It is a day of definitely marked progress in the life of a man when, by the illumination of spirit which proceeds from the development of higher sense of duty, he passes from the burdensome sphere of slavery to the happy world of work; when he leaves behind him the grasping and bartering, the drudgery and humiliation, and, accepting his place among his fellows, becomes a cheerful co-operator with humanity, and a willing and happy instrument in the economy of things.

Such a man receives the completion of wages in its sevenfold fullness as follows:

1. Money
2. Usefulness.
3. Excellence.
4. Power
5. Independence
6. Honor
7. Happiness

First, he receives the full amount of money of which his work is the equivalent; but in addition to this, his usefulness to the world is increased, and continues to increase in an ever ascending degree; and this greater usefulness is one of the pure delights of labor, for one of the chief rewards of use is to be of greater use. To the slave, idleness is coveted as the reward of labor; but the worker rejoices in more work still.

This accumulating usefulness leads to the wages of excellence-skill, a growing perfection in the work undertaken; and every child that has learned its lesson, and every man and woman that has mastered a problem or a language, or surmounted a great difficulty, is acquainted with the happiness which is the sure accompaniment of such success, although not until later do they realize the full significance of all that is involved in such success in relation to their career.

For a point of excellence is at last reached which merges into power-knowledge, mastery. The man who is devoted to his work becomes at last a master in that work, whatever it may be. He becomes a teacher, a guide, and instructor to others who are treading the lower levels of the path up which he has climbed. He is sought out by others for the knowledge which he has acquired through practice and experience. He is relied upon, and takes his proper place amongst those who lead and serve mankind. Power is a form of wages received as the result of long and arduous labor. It is received only by him who has built it up, so to speak, unselfish toil leads to the reaping of power.

Associated with power is independence. The true worker takes his place among his fellows as a useful citizen. The fearless flash of honesty is in his eyes, the ring of worth is in his voice, and the steadfastness of self-reliance is in his gait. He is not a drone in the human hive, but stands out in shining contrast to the skulking shirker who imagines that the highest good in life is to get something without working for it. The slave who goes to his hated work only because he is whipped to it by necessity comes down to beggary and shame, and is despised and neglected; but the true worker ascends into independence and honor, and is admired and sought.

Honor- This is one of the higher forms of wages, and it comes unerringly and unsought to all who are energetic and faithful in the work of their life. It may be, and often is, late in coming, but come it must and does, and always at its own proper time; for while money is the first and smallest item in wages, honor is one of the last and greatest; and the greater the honor, the longer and harder is the course of labor by which it is earned. There are degrees of honor according to the measure of usefulness, and the greatest men receive the greatest honor.

They who receive the fullness of wages, receive the fullness of happiness, for true work as surely brings about happiness as idleness and enforced labor are paid in the coin of unhappiness. From the perfection of happiness proceeds well-being -a quiet conscience, a satisfied heart, a tranquil mind, and the consciousness of having increased the happiness and aided in the progress of mankind through the full and faithful exercise of one's abilities.

First work, and then wages; but well-being only follows when the work is of the true kind, when it is loved for its own sake, and when the money received for such work is utilized for further work and better achievement instead of being squandered in folly and self-indulgence. Even he who only works for the pay in coin will derive just the measure of well-being which that pay can purchase if he spends it carefully, and will thus aid, in a small measure, industrial progress; but he can also, by a foolish use of his wages, make it an instrument of ill-being, and reduce himself to a dead and useless limb on the tree of life.

It is demanded by the law of things that every man shall receive the equivalent of what he gives. If he gives idleness, he receives inactivity- death; if gives stinted and unwilling service, he receives stinted and hardly secured pay; if he gives loving and generous labor, he recipes generous recompense in a life replete with blessedness.

It may here be asked, "But what about the toiling masses? What you say may be, and doubtless is, true of certain favored individuals, but how can it apply to the vast army of millworks and factory hands, whose toil is long and hard and almost purely mechanical?"

It applies with equal force to them. There are no favored individuals; and there was a time when those who now occupy the high places stood in the low. There is no reason why the mill-worker should not be unselfish in his labor and faithful and conscientious in duty; and there is every reason why he should economize his entire financial, physical, and mental resources, using his money for the improvement of his home and surroundings, and his evenings and spare time in the culture of his intellectual and moral powers. He will thus be preparing himself for higher spheres of usefulness and power, which will not be withheld from him when he is sufficiently equipped and strengthened to deal with intricate matters and carry weighty responsibilities; while the process of preparation itself will be one of ever-increasing knowledge, strength, and happiness.

Work, wages, and well-being are three broad stages in individual and racial evolution; and the political economy of the future will take into account those higher mental and spiritual forms of wages which it now ignores, but which are still the most powerful factors in the well-being of men and nations.

Well indeed will it be for that nation which is the first to realize and wisely utilize the fact that its prosperity and happiness are not limited to its material resources, but that in the mental and spiritual material of its inhabitants it possesses inexhaustible mines of living resources which, when worked with the tools of suitably evolved educational methods, will afford rich yields of prosperity and peace; that the surest and swiftest way to even material success as well as to all the higher and nobler successes is by the assiduous cultivation of character.

3. The survival of the fittest as a divine law

NATURE and Spirit were at one time universally considered to be at enmity, and even to-day the majority of people regard them as opposed to each other; but a fuller knowledge of the Cosmos reveals the sublime fact that the natural and the spiritual are two aspects of One Eternal Truth.

Nature is the Spirit made visible and tangible. The seen is the expressed form and letter of the unseen. We search in trackless deserts of speculation to find the Real, while all the time it stands before us. The return from those weary and fruitless wanderings to Truth is a coming back to the simple and obvious; but whereas we went out with sealed eyes, we come back with them unsealed; we look upon Nature with a vision clarified from ignorance and egotism, and lo! the unclean has become clean, the mortal has become immortal, the natural is seen to be also the spiritual. Thus, when the physical scientist reveals a natural law, he, at the same time, makes known to the understanding mind- whether he himself knows it or not- a spiritual law. The whole universe is spiritual, and every physical law is the letter of a moral principle. When the moral nature of the Cosmos is apprehended, all controversies about matter and spirit- as things opposed are at an end, and the assiduous worker in physical realms-often spoken of contemptuously as a "materialist"- is seen to be a revealer, as well as the worker in spiritual realms, the two phases of the universe being, as we have pointed out, but two arcs of one perfect whole.

When Charles Darwin made known the law of "the survival of the fittest," he revealed the working of Divine Justice in Nature. The almost universal prejudice and passionate opposition among religious people which the announcement of his discovery aroused was based, not on the fact itself, but upon a total misunderstanding of that law. That opposition has to-day nearly died out; but even yet one frequently hears this law referred to as a "cruel law", and the belief in it denounced as tending to destroy pity and love.

Such people always think of this law as "the survival of the cruelest," or "the survival of the strongest," and here is where the misunderstanding arises. The correct term, "The Survival of the Fittest," must not be lost sight of; for the fittest are never the cruelest, and rarely the strongest. The strongest and curliest creatures have long since passed away, and have given place to weaker, but more intelligent, creatures and beings. Think of the numberless insects, and of the many powerful enemies which beset them on every hand. Yet these wonderful and beautiful creatures continue to flourish, and they owe their continuance to their intelligence, which is greater, better and more fitted to survive than the strength and cruelty of their enemies. For what is the survival of the fittest but the survival of the best? In a world of continual progress it must needs be that the best of every period takes precedence of the worst-the good of the bad, the fit of the unfit. This, indeed, is the very meaning of progress. When we think of progress, we at once think of something, by its superiority- its greater fitness to the time and occasion-taking precedence f something which is inferior and has fallen out of the line of advancement; and this progress, this advancement, this survival of the fittest, resolves itself into a moral principle, into a Divine Law.

Opponents of this teaching tacitly assume that the most selfish are the fittest to survive, and they thereupon condemn the teaching as callous, and accuse Darwin of making selfishness supreme. But the error is theirs, and not Darwin's or the law's. In their prejudice they wrest his meaning to a false issue, and attack that. Their error consists in assuming that the fittest to survive are the most selfish; whereas such are the worst specimens, and not the best. When we realize that the unselfish are more fitted to survive than the selfish, this law assumes an aspect the very opposite from that which its opponents have given it, and we at once see that in it are involved the profoundest moral principles, namely, the principles of Justice and Love.

Remembering that it is the fittest that survive, what, then-in this universe of law and order-constitutes the fittest? It is evident that the fittest are the most advanced specimens of any given species. Not the strongest, not the cruelest, not the most selfish, not even the finest physically; but the most advanced, those most in line with the order of evolution

The fittest at one period are not the fittest at another. There was a time when brute force was dominant; but that was when nothing higher had been evolved. Yet even in that long distant period-ten million years back, when gigantic monsters held sway upon the earthy-something higher was being evolved. Already intelligence, yea, and unselfish love, were beginning to make themselves felt, for those great beasts loved and protected their young; and so all who most unselfishly shield their offspring, be they beasts or men, will be most protected while, obviously, any species that neglected its offspring would rapidly perish. Thus, long, long ages ago, the fragile babe of intelligence was born in the manager of brute force, and since then, through all the ages of struggle, it has been gradually but surely overcoming the brutal strength and terror; so that to-day intelligence has conquered, or almost conquered, for the strongest brutes have passed away for ever, having given place to beings physically weaker and smaller, but better, and more morally perfect.

Without the operation of such a law man could never have come into existence; for man is, up to the present, the crown and summit of a process of struggle, selection, and progress which began many millions of years ago when the first of life appeared upon the earth. Man is the product of the law of the survival of the fittest operating through millions of years, perhaps millions of ages; yet in brute strength he is far inferior to many animals. He rules the earth to-day because of the principle of intelligence within him. But there is being evolved in man a higher principle than intelligence, namely, Divine Love, which is as much higher and more powerful than intelligence as intelligence is higher and more powerful than brute force. I use the term "Divine Love" in order to distinguish it from human affection, and from that intermittent kindly impulse, which are both spoken of as Love. Intelligence may aid selfishness, but not so Love; in Love all selfishness is swallowed up and brute force is no more, both being transmuted into gentleness.

The beginnings of the Divine Love are already in the world. We see its wonderful operation in the few men in who0m it has been perfected, namely, the Great Spiritual Teachers who, by their precepts and the example of their lives, rule the world to-day; and selfish men worship them as God. We see in these men the prophecy of what Love will do in the distant future, when a large number of men possess it in an advanced degree; how selfishness and selfish men will submit to it and be governed by it, as the brutes now submit to man's intelligence and are ruled by it. And this Love is making its appearance not only in the Great Teachers, but in men less evolved; and though in these it is, as yet, in a more or less rudimentary form, nevertheless the stirrings of its gentleness and joy are being felt in many human hearts.

A common argument against the survival of the fittest is that were men to put it into practice they would kill off all their weakling and invalids, preserving only the strong, and thus destroying all pity and love and humanity. This argument is a demonstration of the error to which we have already referred. It is ludicrously self-contradictory, for, while it admits that the best elements are pity and love and humanity, it asserts that these would perish if the fittest, or best survived. And here we are at the heart of the whole matter. The best does survive, and, therefore, pity, compassion, and love cannot be overthrown by selfishness is for every annihilated.

Speaking of human beings, it is plain that the fittest to survive are not the selfish and the cruel, but those who have developed the finest characteristics of kindness, compassion, justice, and love- in a word, the most moral, the purest, and wisest.

To talk about putting this law "into practice" shows ignorance of its nature; for it is independent in its operation, and is always in activity, and all men and creatures obey it; and should ever a race of men, under them is taken notion that they were practicing it, do it such violence as to "kill off their weaklings and invalids," the law would not cease to operate in their case, and they, by virtue of that very law, would soon exterminate themselves.

With the ceaseless march of human progress, cruelty is becoming less and less fitted to survive against the growing intelligence and gentleness. The cruel races have nearly all died out, only disorganized remnants of them remaining. The fierce animals of prey are becoming fewer, and brutal men are now regarded as a menace to society. Gradually and inevitably, also, selfish and aggressive men will come to have less and less power in the world, will become more out of harmony with the growing environment of peace and goodwill, till at last they will pass away from the earth altogether, as the gigantic brutes have passed away, no longer fitted to survive in a world conquered by Love, in which righteousness and truth become triumphant.

Thus this law, as represented by Darwin, is the aspect, in Nature, of the operation of Justice, or Love; for in the Light of Truth, Justice and Love are seen to be one. The spiritual aspect of the law was intimately known by all the Great Teachers, and men have overlooked the fact that these Teachers embodied it in their teaching. Thus the precept of Jesus, "The meek shall inherit the earth," is none other than a simple but Divine statement of the survival of the fittest.

4. Justice in evil

TO-DAY we frequently meet with the assertion, "All is good." Pope, in his famous easy on man, said:

"Whatever is, is right"

and nearly all are familiar with Browing's oft-quoted line:

"God's in His heaven, all's right with the world."

In the face of these statements, the questions naturally arise: Are war and famine good? Are sickness and poverty good? Are sorrow and suffering good? These things belong to the category of the great facts of human life; are they good? Again, are sin and selfishness right? Are drunkenness and brutality right? Are crime and violence right? Are accidents by sea and land right? Are catastrophes involving hundreds of thousands of lives right? These things, like the former, are everyday facts. They are real, and cause widespread suffering; are they right?

Many persons must have questioned thus during the past years of unprecedented catastrophes in the form of volcanic eruptions, earthy quakes, floods, famines, wars, and various forms of crimes and violence.

Are these things right? If so, why are men so eager to escape them? Even those who are given to quoting, "Whatever is, is right," will, in the next breath, refer to certain "evils," and propose some method of being rid of them.

It is plain that, in the sense of adding to human happiness, these things are not right, for they conduce to human misery. Even those who deny the existence of evil in theory recognize it in practice, in their efforts to conquer it.

Nevertheless, those statements as to the Universal Good and the rightness of all things are true. It is all a matter of relativity. The recognition of evil, and the statement that all is good, are not contradictory. When the events of life are related to human happiness, then some are recognized as "good," and some as "evil"; but when they are related to the fundamental and eternal principle of Justice, then all things are seen to be good, right, in harmony with the Great Law of inviolable Equity.

Take a simple example-that of physical pain. When we are considering human happiness, bodily pain is an evil; but when we consider the principle of Life itself, and its protection and continuance, then physical pain is seen to be good, as it is a warning. Monitor urging man to the protection of his body from hurt and extinction.

And it is with mental pain as with physical-with sorrow, remorse, loneliness, and grief it is evil because it destroys happiness; but as the effect of ignorance and wrong-doing, it is just, and therefore good, as it urges men to seek the paths of wisdom and right doing.

The prophet Isaiah says:

"I form the light, and create darkness; I make peace, and create evil: I the Lord do all these things."

He thus recognizes the justice of evil, that it has its place in the moral universe as the opposite of good, just as darkness has its place in the physical universe as the opposite of light.

The prophet Amos expresses the same thing when he says:

"Shall there be evil in a city, and the Lord hat not done it?"

The writings of the Hebrew prophets in the Old Testament teem with statement of the truth that evil is rooted in justice, not in injustice; that all the afflictions and calamities which overtake men spring from some violation, on man's part, of the moral law. So pronounced are they upon this point that they even attribute the suffering caused by purely external occurrences - such as floods, storms, earthquakes, drought, and dearth of food-to man's inward unrighteousness and his consequent departure from the Divine Order.

And, indeed, a profound acquaintance with the human heart and with human life does reveal the great truth-a truth never apparent on the surface, and therefore hidden from the shallow and unthinking-that all tragedy is the culminating point in the conflict of human passions. Where there are no violent passions there can be no tragedy, no disaster, no catastrophe. When humanity has attained to inward harmony and peace, it will be free from all those forms of violence which now devastate the world, and scourge humankind with grief and lamentation.

Maeterlinck perceives this truth clearly, for in his Wisdom and Destiny he says:

> *"Fatality shrinks back abashed from the soul that has more than once conquered her; there are certain disasters she dare not send forth when this soul is near.*
>
> *"The mere presence of the sage suffices to paralyze destiny; and of this we find proof in the fact that there exists scarce a drama wherein a true sage appears; when such is the case, the event must needs halt before reaching bloodshed and tears. Not only is there no drama wherein sage is in conflict with sage, but indeed there are very few whose action revolves round a sage. And truly; can we imagine that an event shall turn into tragedy between men who have earnestly striven to gain knowledge of self? It is rarely indeed that though it be for an instant. They are afraid of a lofty soul, for they know that events are no less afraid; and were there heroes to soar to the height the real hero would gain, their weapons would fall to the ground, and the drama itself become peace - the peace of enlightenment."*

It is a significant fact that while Shakespeare depicted nearly every type of character, he never brought a sage into his dramas. The truth is that his tragedies could not have taken place in the presence of a sage. Their outward violence stands related as effect to the hidden cause of disordered and conflicting passions. The sage has lifted himself above such disorder and conflict, and such is the power of his harmonious and tranquil spirit that in his presence the passions of others will be calmed and subdued, and their approaching tragic issue averted.

It is a mighty truth, and one which stands clearly revealed in the mind of the sage and the prophet, that all the evils of humanity spring from the ignorance, and, therefore, from the mistakes, the wrong-doing, of humanity itself. It is, therefore, just and right. But though just and right, it is not desirable; it is evil, and needs to be transcended. It is just and right, as imprisonment is just and right for the thief, in that it teaches man, and ultimately brings him to the feet of wisdom. As physical pain is a protector of man's body, so mental pain is a protector of his mind and of his life.

From man's ignorance of the Divine Law-of the Moral Order of the universe-arise those thoughts and passions-inward conditions-which are the source of tragedy, disaster, catastrophe. Envy, ill-will, jealousy, produce strife and quarrelling, and ultimately bring about wars in which thousands are killed and disabled, and hundreds of homes are filled with mourning. Greediness, self-indulgence, and the thirst for pleasure lead, through gluttony, indolence, and drunkenness, to disease, poverty, and plague. Covetousness, lust, and selfishness in all its forms cause men to practice deception, lying, and dishonesty, and to strive against others in the blind pursuance of their petty plans and pleasures, thus leading to deprivation, loss and ruin; and where there are excessively violent passions there is always a violent life ending in a premature and violent death.

Man, by his ignorance, his selfishness, his darkness of mind, is the marker of sorrow and the cause of catastrophe. His sufferings are indications that the Divine Law has been arrested, and is now asserting itself. The tragic darkness of his life is the outcome of that same Justice from which his joyful light proceeds. If every suicide, every ruin, every woe, even every accident, could be traced to its original cause in the moral constitution of things, its justice would be found to be without blemish.

And that which applies to individuals applies in the same way to nations. Widespread selfishness leads inevitably to widespread disaster; national corruption is followed by wholesale catastrophe, and by national disaster and ruin.

And not alone poverty, disease, and famine, but even earthquakes, volcanic eruptions, floods and all such external happenings, would be found, in their original cause, to be intimately related to men's moral life. That external accidents have a moral cause is plainly seen in the case of violent persons bringing about fatal accidents to themselves through folly and recklessness.

Man's body, both by chemical and gravitational affinity, is a portion of the earth, as his mind, both spiritually and ethically, is a portion of the Moral Order of the universe. His life and being are interwoven with, and are inseparable from; the very nature and constitution of things; and, being a moral entity, and therefore a reasonable agent, it is within the domain of his power to discover and work with the Divine Law instead of striving against it.

All man's pains, afflictions, disasters, calamities, are the shock resulting from running, either percipiently or blindly, giants the Moral Law, as a reckless rider or blind man is hurt when he runs up against a wall; and these sorrows are not the arbitrary visitations and punishments of an offended Deity, but are matters of cause and effect, just as the pain of burning is the effect of coming into too close contact with fire.

In these days of social, political, and theological conflicts, and with wars, famines, floods, crimes, conflagrations, and volcanic and seismic catastrophes taking place on every hand, a return to the study of the Hebrew prophets burning, as they are, with the fire of Truth on national matters and local catastrophes-would prove not only scientifically enlightening, but would help considerably towards unveiling, in the mind of man, the revelation of the beauty and order of the Cosmos and the perfect justice of human life.

The evils of life are right because of the cause which man has created; but man, having created causes which produce evil, can also create causes which produce good, and when in inward passions are tamed and subdued, the outward violence will disappear, or will be powerless to hurt mankind.

Between the inward violence of surging passions and the outward violence of Nature there is such a close correspondence as to render them, in the inner order of things, of one indivisible essence. As the prophet Amos again puts it:

"For they know not to do right, faith the Lord, who store up violence and robbery in their places. Therefore thus faith the Lord God: An adversary there shall be even round

about the land; and he shall bring down they strength from thee, and thy places shall be spooled."

The outward "adversary" is necessary to nullify the inward violence, is brought into existence by it. When a nation becomes corrupt, it is conquered and swallowed up. When cities become morally bankrupt, they fall to pieces, or are destroyed by some outward force.

5. Justice and love

ONE frequently hears justice referred to as being opposed to love. Such an error arises out of lack of understanding of the profound and comprehensive significance of these two principles, for two divine laws cannot stand in opposition or contradiction to each other. Two basic laws, both admittedly good, must harmonize; otherwise one would be evil, for good cannot oppose good. The antagonism which men place between justice and love does not exist in reality; it is an error arising from ignorance of the true nature and right application of the principles involved.

The element of kindness is never absent from justice; if it were, it would be weak emotionalism and not love. There is often more love in a server reproof than in a yielding acquiescence. The father who has little love for his child, though he may not treat it cruelly, will not take pains to train it properly; but the father who has great love for his child will train it with a firm yet gentle hand. He will be just to his child because he loves it. He will administer correction and reproof when necessary, that his child may profit thereby.

Justice is not separate from love; love is not separate from justice. The essential oneness of the two principles is simply expressed in the divine edict: "Whatsoever a man swath, that shall he also reap." It is in accordance both with perfect love and perfect justice that man should reap the good results of his good deeds, and the bad results of his bad deeds. All men admit this theoretically, though the majority refuse to recognize the operation of such a law in the universe, arguing, when overtaken with trouble, that in their case they are not reaping what they have sown, as they have never done anything to call for such misfortune, but are suffering innocently (unjustly), or are afflicted through the wrong-doing of others.

Such a law, however, obtains, and those who will search long enough, and look deep below the surface of things, will find it, and be able to trace with precision its faultless working. Nor would a right-minded man wish it to be otherwise. He would know that the kindest thing that could be done to him would be that he should suffer the full penalty of all his mistakes and wrong-doing, so that he might thereby grow more rapidly in virtue and wisdom. Petitions to Deity to abrogate the just punishment of sins committed are without avail, and can only spring from an immature moral sense. Woe indeed would descend upon man if the law of justice could thus be set aside.

Self-afflicted and torn with sorrow as he now is, there is hope in the law which bestows no special favors and is unfailingly just. But if man by offering up a prayer could escape the effects of his bad deeds, then justice would be non-existent; and as for love, where would it be? For if one could thus be deprived of his bad earnings, what assurance could he have of not being robbed of his good earnings? Thus the ground of salvation would be cut away, and caprice and despotism would take the place of love and justice.

As a coin, which is one, has two distinct sides, so love and justice are two aspects of the same thing. Men do not perceive the love that is hidden in justice, nor the justice that hidden love, because they perceive only one side, and do not to turn these principles round, as it were, and see them in their completion.

Justice, being a divine principle, cannot contain any element of cruelty. All its apparent harshness is the chastening fire of love. Man himself, and not the law per se, has brought about all the afflictions which are working for his ultimate happiness and good. Love reigns supreme in the universe because justice is supreme. A tender and loving hand administers the rod of chastisement. Man is protected, even against himself. Love and justice are one.

6. Self-protection: animal, human, and divine

MANY and wonderful are the means and methods of self-protection in this world of combat! Natural history has revealed the fact that even plants employ means of self-protection; and when we come to the animal world, the methods adopted to avoid annihilation in the struggle for life are so numerous and remarkable as to call forth our admiration and wonder. Nor in this fight for life is "the battle to the fierce and the race to the strong" in all cases. Indeed, the weak things of nature exhibit such ingenuity in the means which they adopt to escape their enemies, that they are equally successful in holding their own with the fiercest creatures that have few enemies to fear. The insects, weakest of all creatures, have developed this self-protective ingenuity to a remarkable degree, even to imitating in color and form the twinges upon which they rest, adopting the hue of the soil or the dead or living leaves among which they live; and in some cases, through long experience, they have so closely imitated in color and form certain flowers which they habitually haunt that their enemies the birds, keen as is their sight, pass them by; and even man, with all his intelligence, cannot distinguish them from the flowers unless he had had some experience as an observant naturalist. The smallest fishes adopt similar means of concealing themselves, although they are in the lowest class of animal life.

When we come to the quadrupeds (although the weaker and smaller among them, those most hunted by the larger, adopt ruses similar to those which prevail among the insects and fishes), brute strength largely takes the place of stratagem. The beast has developed powerful weapons of defense, such as horns, fangs, claws &c., combined with an iron or lithe muscularity, with which he maintains his place on the earth, and defies extinction. Endurance, speed, strength, and ferocity are the means of self-protection among the brutes.

Animal self-protection reaches its highest excellence in the superb strength and cunning of the lion and the tiger, yet it appears weak and clumsy when compared with the means of self-protection adopted by man; for self-preservation, although it is not all-powerful in the human as in the animal world is still a dominant impulse among human beings. Man is possessed of the entire animal nature and the animal impulses and instincts are strong within him; but there is along with this animal life an added intelligence and moral sense-a self-consciousness -- by virtue of which his self-protective scope and power are greatly enlarged and intensified. He is still an animal, with endurance, speed, strength, and ferocity; but he is also something more and greater-he is an intelligent, self-conscious being.

Among men of low order of intelligence the animal methods still largely obtain. In the struggle of life the savage relies on brute strength. Even among civilized communities there are still thousands of admirers of "the noble art of self-defense," which can only be noble in the sense that we speak of the ferocity of the lion as being noble; and is devoid of art, being compounded entirely of brute force and cunning. Indeed, this practice is so closely allied to the beast that it has long ceased to be a means of self-defense among civilized men, and has become merely a vulgar pastime for the few.

Working along physical lines, and still following the well-worn track of animal instinct, man has invented numerous implements of destruction by which to annihilate his enemy and preserve himself; and upon these, with increasing ingenuity and subtlety, he continues to improve. Working along the new path of pure intelligence-which is pre-eminently the human as distinguished from the animal sphere of activity-he discovers means of adding to his physical comforts and for the peaceful protection of his body, and asserts his right and power to live, not by brute force, but by toil of hand and keenness of brain. The basic struggle here, indeed, is not directly a fight for food and life, but for the artificial means by which food is procured and life maintained, namely, money. The fierce animal struggle has evolved into the more kindly human one; in place of the bloody strife with tooth and claw there is the more amicable combat of wit and skill. Man has discovered- though he has as yet only partially learned this- that there are better methods of self-protection than that of attacking, killing, and despoiling others; that by such a method he endangers his own comfort, happiness, and even life; and that it is better to engage in a bloodless competition for supremacy, and leave every person to take his place in life according to the measure of his mental capacity.

Right has begun to take the place of might; and although the struggle is largely one for money, it is not altogether so, but is surely evolving into one for the securing of those mental qualities which increase man's nobility, and better fit him as an instrument of life and progress. Such are the intellectual qualities of reason, judgement, tact, foresight, ingenuity, resource, inventiveness; and the moral qualities of kindness, forbearance, sympathy, forgiveness, reverence, honesty, justice. Human education at present is almost entirely along these intellectual and moral lines. The instruments by which man struggles with man for the capacity to live and to endure are faculties, not fangs; talents, not talons.

Intellectual and moral excellence constitute the passport to existence in the human world.

The intellectually vigorous and the morally upright take the lead in the race of life. Nevertheless, the weaker ones take their place, and have scope and opportunity for development. Slowly man is learning that in the protection of others- the weak, the suffering, and the afflicted-he is affording a surer protection for himself.

Such methods of self-protection we perceive an enormous advance upon the savage instinct of the brute. Commerce, crafts, and games take the place of plunder and destruction; and limited animal affection is enlarged to benevolence and philanthropy. In human competition the brute still lurks, but its ferocity is subdued; its nature is largely transmuted into something better, more beneficent; its dark horror is lightened up with the warm rays of kindness; its harshness is softened by the gentleness of a larger and ever-increasing love.

But high as is human over animal self-protection, there is another, form of self-protection that is as high above the human as that is above the animal, and that is divine or spiritual protection. By this method the man does not fight with others physically, after the manner of the brute; he does not struggle with others mentally, as does the human being; he fights with the brute within himself, in order to annihilate it; he struggles with the greed in his own nature, that he may fit himself to live the higher, nobler, more enduring life of peace, goodwill, and wisdom.

In divine protection the fierce struggle with others is at and end, the competition of self-interest is no more, and the weapons employed are self-sacrifice and non-resistance. And these weapons can only be understood and employed by him whose moral elevation is such as to gain him admittance to the World of Divine Things. Just as the fanged and tallied brute cannot grasp and use those mental weapons of resource and inventiveness which the more highly endowed and talented human being employs with such ease and power, so the self-seeking man cannot comprehend and wield those instruments of self-sacrifice and non-resistance with which the divine man not merely shields himself but protects the whole world.

Self-interest, resistance to, and competition with others, are the most powerful factors in the purely human life; but in the divine life, self-obliteration, and deep-felt sympathy with, and compassion for others, are the dominant motives.

The divine man conquers by non-retaliation and by yielding where others enter into selfish strife; and his gentle powers are so invincible that the lesser selfish powers, great and potent as those are when compared with the merely animal equipment's, dissolve away in ineffectual weakness. As bestial instincts cannot vie with human powers, so human powers cannot stand against divine principles; and the divine man stands upon, and acts from, such principles. In him the human qualities mentioned are merged into the divine principles of Patience, Humility, Purity, Compassion, and Love.

Both the animal and the human are concerned only with the protection and preservation of the body, which is temporal; but the divine man's preservation is concerned with the spirit, which is eternal, like the principles upon which he stands. In a word, divine preservation consists in preserving the mind from passion and selfishness, and imbuing it with pureness and wisdom.

We get a glimpse into the vast power inherent in self-sacrifice and non-resistance when we contemplate the lives and characters of the few divine men who practiced these principles - in Jesus, Buddha, and others. All men, broadly speaking, yield and bow down to these great Masters in Divine Things. Men who have reached the greatest heights in worldly achievement- monarchs, conquerors, successful generals, statesmen, orators, financiers- bow in humble reverence and awe before the names of those Great Ones, recognizing intuitively that their own conquests and achievements, with all their worldly glory, are as nothing compared with that supreme self-conquest, that mighty spiritual achievement, which those gentle teachers of mankind exhibited. To-day some five hundred millions of people bow down to Buddha as their Guide and Master, and some three hundred millions likewise bend before Jesus as their Saviour and the Keeper of their lives.

In these three methods of self-protection-animal, human, and spiritual-we perceive the fundamental forces which are at work in the evolution of sentient beings; an evolution beginning with the lowest creature and extending to the deviants being of whom we have any direct knowledge. We also see that there is no inherent evil in any of these methods, that all are equally legitimate, and belong to the cosmic order of things. Each in its own sphere is right and necessary, leading to higher and higher intelligence, and deeper and deeper knowledge. The animal defends itself in accordance with its nature and the limits of its knowledge; the human being protects itself likewise in harmony with the dictates of his human nature; and the divine being eternally preserves himself in peace and blessedness by virtue of his clearer insight and deeper wisdom.

Nor is any measure of force lost during the process of evolution. The brute passion is, in man, transmuted into intellectual and moral energy, and in the divine man both are merged into control and equanimity.

7. Aviation and the new consciousness

DR. BUCKE, in his work Cosmic Consciousness, published some ten years ago, stated that aerial navigation would become an accomplished fact in the near future, and that it would revolutionize the social and economic conditions of the world.

So far as the advent of the new means of travel is concerned, he has proved to be a true prophet, and i am convinced that his prophecy of its revolutionizing aspect will shortly begin to be proved true. Of this great revolution in its completion Dr. Bucke says:

"Before aerial navigation boundaries, tariffs, and perhaps, distinctions of language will fade out. Great cities will no longer have reason for being, and will melt away. The men who now dwell in cities will inhabit, in summer, the mountains and the sea shores; building often in airy and beautiful spots, now almost or quite inaccessible, commanding the most extensive and magnificent views. In the winter they will probably dwell in communities of moderate size. As the herding together, as now, in great cities, so the isolation of the worker of the soil will become a thing of the past. Space will be practically annihilated; there will be no crowding together and no enforced solitude."

The above is a beautiful picture of the result upon human society of the discovery of aviation, and it will no doubt prove true. Not that such a condition will be brought about rapidly. It will at least require several hundred years, and it is highly probable that it will be several thousand years before it is fully realized. As yet we are only in the crudest beginnings of flying, and the mastery of the air as a medium of human transit affords more scope for improvement and invention than any of the mechanical modes of locomotion hitherto employed. Invention will follow upon invention, through a long period of time, until men will be able to propel themselves through the air with a swiftness, a safety, and a skill perhaps equal to that of the migratory birds for the swiftest type. It was Edison who long years ago declared that the ultimate and perfected flying-machine would be built on the principle of the bird. While conforming more or less to this principle, the present machines are more on the principle of the kite, the motor-driving power taking the place of the string. In his book The Coming Race Lord Lytton describes the individuals of that race as each possessing a pair of mechanical wings which were under the complete control of the operator, and by means of which he soared into their and propelled himself gracefully through space. Doubtless this will be form which the perfected flying-machine will take, and it conforms to that "principle of the bird" referred to by Edison.

But the phase of aviation with which we are here concerned is that which connects it with the evolving consciousness of man; for out of that self-consciousness, which is now man's dominant condition, and which is inevitably connected with struggle and suffering, with labor and sorrow, the beginnings of a higher, diviner form of consciousness are making their appearances. From man's present state of imperfection, combined with ceaseless aspiration towards a better, but as yet undefined, state, there is surely coming, as form a matrix, a new order of life, a more blessed condition, a greatly evolved form of consciousness hitherto unknown to man except in a few isolated cases.

Invention is allied to progress-is, indeed, an outward manifestation of inward growth. All man's inventions are adaptations to his expanding consciousness, and they definitely mark important turning-points in the evolution of the race. At the moment man's necessity the new and needed thing appears. Just as the human intellect was preparing to break from the bonds of old superstitions, and sally forth in joyous and untrammeled freedom, the printing press appeared as the chief instrument of man's liberation. The coming of the steam engine tallied with the accelerated speed of human thought as it began to shake off its ancient lethargy; and when the expanding human mind could no longer move in a contracted local circle, or remain satisfied with petty selfish differences, the locomotive came forth to meet man's wider range, and to afford him scope for his increased mental activities and enlarged sympathies.

And now another invention has entered the field of actuality; one growing out of, yet more important than, any which have preceded it- that of flying. Man has hitherto employed the solid earth and the less solid water as the medium of material transit; but now he is to make and obedient servant of the tenuous atmosphere, using it to speed bird-like directly to his desired destination. And this is an important outward sign of the new stride in evolution which the race is now taking. Rapid and restless changes are marking the present transition period. Old religions and forms of government are passing away. New modes of thought and action are everywhere appearing. Man's consciousness is expanding. The human form of consciousness is about to touch, is indeed touching, the point of completion, and from it there will spring, is already springing, the Divine form of consciousness which is destined to transform the entire human race. For under that the reign of consciousness nearly everything, as it at present obtains in the world, will be reversed. Man, being then Divine, will act divinely. All those powerful human passions which now dominate the race, and are the chief springs of action, will then take a subordinate place, and will be under the control and guidance of man's Divine will and wisdom. He will be master of himself and master of the earth.

Already man has been feeling the growing wings of this new consciousness wherewith he will soar into the highest regions of knowledge and blessedness. For ages, and under the guise of numerous religions, he has aspired to it, and the prophets have foretold it, and now he is to obtain his Divine birthright.

Aviation is the first outward symbol, as it were, of this new mind which is now taking shape. It is also more than a symbol, for its will form the first important material instrument by the aid of which the new consciousness will begin to materialize its glorious ideas and magnificent schemes for the happiness of to-day is misery compared with that blessed state which will obtain on the earth when the Divine condition has become well established.

The beginnings of this new condition, as aided by aviation, will be noticed in the breaking down of certain material limitations between man and man, and between nations, and the disappearance of war; along with it will come a free and fraternal industrial intercourse between the nations, and a growing tendency to adopt in practice those fundamental religious principles which are universal, and thus to inaugurate one great world-wide religion. As aviation becomes more perfected, and enters into man's economical schemes, these new conditions-the first seedlings, as it were, of the new consciousness-will begin to appear, for when men are rapidly fitting from country to country, from continent to continent, on "the wings of the wind," they will be brought so close together, both socially and industrially, that the old animosities which now exist between them will die out, the old national barriers will quietly break down and disappear, and, without any revolutionary upheaval, the nations will become as one country, sinking all those interests which are not for the mutual good of all nations.

The locomotive is an instance of the above, though in the region of self-consciousness, in that it rendered civil war impossible, making of each nation, formerly dividend against itself, a united family working harmoniously together. Aviation, however, will be connected with a higher region of consciousness altogether, namely, the cosmic consciousness, and its results will be much more striking and more far-reaching than those which have hitherto taken place in man's self-conscious condition.

At present we are only in the experimental stage of aviation, but this will be quickly followed by the economic stage, in which flying will be adapted to human travel and mercantile uses; and almost immediately this is reached the new conditions is societies and nations will begin to manifest themselves, and once having commenced they will gradually absorb the old forms of life, using them as material on which to feed their growing beauty and grandeur. And new and grand men will arise having this higher consciousness, and they will be the leading instruments in establishing this new order of things upon the earth.

8. The new courage

THE virtue of courage is generally referred to in its physical manifestation, and it is significant in this particular- that its symbol is a beast of prey, namely, the lion. The dictionary rendering adheres to this physical aspect of courage, for on turning up the word I find its meanings are given as "bravery, fearlessness, intrepidity," no other rendering being given. The solider is the human type of courage, and the current sayings concerning courage are: "As courageous as a lion" and "As brave as a solider."

The lion and the solider are alike fearless in attack and defense, and both will forfeit life rather than yield; but it is an entirely animal physical attack and defense. Courage, however, cannot be confined to this phase-indeed, this is its lowest manifestation -for it has many aspects, many modes of action; and as man rises in the moral and spiritual scale his courage becomes transmuted, taking a newer and higher form. But before proceeding to the highest form of courage, which is the subject of this article, it is necessary that the lower forms should be first considered.

With the physical form of courage already referred to all are familiar. It is common both to animals and men. It arises in fearlessness. Its twofold mode of action is attack and defense. It will be seen, however, that this kind of courage is inevitably associated with suffering, even with destruction and death, as daily manifested both in the animal and human spheres of life; self-protection being its dominant motive, whether in attack or defense.

But man is not only and merely an animal, a physical being; he is also a moral and intellectual being; and along with his moral evolution he began to develop a higher kind of courage-not the highest, or the New Courage herein referred to; but yet a great advance on the purely animal courage, namely, moral courage. In physical courage the other person's body or property is attacked, while one's own body or property is defended. In moral courage the other person's ideas, opinions, or principles are attacked, one's own ideas, opinions, and principles being defended. There is the same fearlessness, the same attack and defense so far as the spirit of courage is concerned; but as regards its letter, these conditions have undergone a change; their physical aspect has disappeared, and, having undergone a process of transmutation, has reappeared in a new form, for moral courage is concerned not with persons as persons, but with their principles. It is, indeed, purely mental; and while it is still concerned with destruction and is associated with suffering, the destruction is a bloodless and intellectual one, namely, the destruction of other men's opinions, and its suffering is mental and not physical.

This form of courage is now generally recognized, and is always referred to as moral courage, to distinguish it from common or physical courage. It is, without doubt, a comparatively recent development in the evolution of the race, and is entirely absent from animals. A few thousand years ago it was, in all probability, an exceeding rare and new faculty, and it is still in process of development, large numbers of the race not yet having evolved it; for while it is probable that at least seventy-five per cent of the race possess a considerable development of physical courage, it is doubtful whether twenty per cent possess any marked degree of moral courage; so much so that those in full possession of it are marked off from their fellows as men of a higher grade of character, and generally- though not necessarily and always- as leaders of men in their particular sphere of action.

But the New Courage, up to a consideration of which the preceding remarks have been leading, is a still higher form of courage- is, indeed, as much above and beyond moral courage as moral courage is above and beyond physical courage; and is as separate and distinct from it as that is from its precedent form. I have called it the New Courage because it is now new in the race, its manifestation being at present very rare, and, therefore, little understood. Though very different from moral courage, it results from it, just as moral courage, though very different from physical courage, though very different from physical courage results from it. Physical courage is of the animal; moral courage is of the human; the New Courage is of the Divine. The new Courage is, therefore, Divine fearlessness as distinguished from animal or human fearlessness.

This Divine fearlessness has a twofold aspect. It at first consists in fearlessly attacking and overcoming the enemies within one's own mind-instead of the enemies without, as in the other two forms of courage- and is afterwards characterized by an entirely new method of conduct towards others, especially where external enmity and opposition have to be met. It is its latter and perfected stage with which we are here concerned - that is, with its outward manifestation.

We have seen how a man having physical courage acts in defense of his life and property; also how a man having moral courage acts in defense of his opinions; and now, how does one act who has Divine courage?

He who has the New Courage does not attack other men or defend himself; does not attack their opinions or defend his own; he is the defender of all men, and that from which he defends them is their own folly, their own ungoverned passions. While never seeking to protect himself, he so acts as to shield others from their deadliest enemy, namely, the evil within themselves.

Both physical and moral courage make much noise. In the one there is the clash of arms and the roar of artillery, along with the shouts of the victories and the groans of the dying; in the other there is the fierce war of opinions and the clamor of conflicting tongues. But in the New Courage there is a profound silence; yet this silence has more influence and enduring power in one man than that noise has in entire humanity. The New Courage may, indeed be described as the courage to be silent. Thus, when the man of Divine courage is attacked, abused, or slandered, he remains serenely silent. Yet this is not a proud and selfish silence. It is a silence based upon a right knowledge of life and having a profound and beneficent purpose; that purpose being the good of the attacking person (and, through him, of all mankind) by protecting him from the evil passion by which he is so injuriously influenced.

To remain silent, calm, and compassionate in the midst of a seething sea of human passions externally pressing upon one-to achieve this requires a lofty courage such as is yet almost unknown to men; so much so that the few men who have it, although misunderstood and persecuted through life, are afterwards worshiped by mankind as Divine and miraculous beings. And here we see how this courage continues to operate even after its possessor is gone from mortal vision. The physically courageous man conquers another in fight; the morally courageous man conquers the opinions of many men, and wins thousands to his cause; but the divinely courageous man conquers the world, and his conquest is one of blessedness and peace, and not of bloodshed or party strife.

In the New Courage, attack and defense, and they obtain in the two lower kinds of courage, have entirely disappeared. Nevertheless, they have not been destroyed; they still exist in the sporty, but have become blended into one, have been transmuted into a sublime and universal kindness; for when the Divine man refrains from engaging in combat with his adversary, and lets him go feeling that he has all the victory, it is because his thought is all for his mistaken enemy, and not for his own defense. He is prompted by a profound compassion for his enemy, a compassion based on Divine and perfect knowledge; and if his silent act does not always subdue the passions of his adversary at the time being, it subdues the passions of thousands of men through hundreds of future generations merely by its recital, so great and far-reaching is the power of one deed of truth.

In the New Courage, then, silent kindness (and by this meant something vastly different from that human impulse commonly called kindness) is both attack and defense. Instead of attempting to conquer passion by fiercer passion - which is the human way- it conquers it, and far more successfully, by it's opposite, namely, gentleness, which is the Divine way. In the human sense, passion is not opposed at all, but is left alone; yet, in reality, it is opposed by something far more powerful than passion, for in all combats between Divine gentleness and human passion gentleness is the supreme victor. Thus, the man of Divine courage, while, viewed from the lower standards of bravery, is not protecting or defending himself, and may for the time being be regarded as a coward, is, in reality, defending himself far more perfectly and successfully than the passionate fighters and partisans; for he who protects his enemy with love, and shields all men with the acts of Divine gentleness, is throwing around himself an eternal shield and protection.

For instances of this New Courage one has to go to the Great Spiritual Leaders of the race, so rare is it. The most striking instance is that of Jesus, who, when mocked, smitten, and crucified, did not retaliate, or offer the least resistance, or speak a world in self-defense; and the fact that the rabble taunted Him with the accusation, "He saved others, Himself He cannot save," seems to show that they regarded Him both as an impostor and a coward. Think of the sublime courage required to pass through such an ordeal, and you will have some conception as to how far the New Courage transcends the ordinary human forms of bravery. That transcendent act of courage, too, is to-day universally recognized as Divine, and it still continues to lift men above their warring, selfish passions.

When the Buddha was abused and falsely accused by His enemies, He always remained silent; and it not infrequently happened that those who came as accusing enemies went away as worshiping friends and disciples, so powerful was His silent gentleness.

It will be long, as we count time, before such courage becomes general in the race; but everything is making towards it. Other men will come who possess it, and then more an more, until at last the race will stand at this Divine level. Then selfishness and sorrow will be ended, and the painful conflict of human passions will no more be heard upon earth.

The Shining Gateway

Editor's foreword

Students of the works of James Allen all over the world will welcome with joy another book from his able pen. In this work we find the *Prophet of Meditation* in one of his deepest and yet most lucid expositions. How wonderfully he deals with fundamental principles ! Here the reader will find no vague statement of generalities, for the writer enters with tender reverence into every detail of human experience. It is as though he came back to *The Shining Gate,* and, standing there, he reviewed all the way up which his own feet have travelled, passing over no temptation that is common to man; knowing that the obstacles that barred his ascending pathway, or the clouds that at times obscured his vision, are the common experiences of all those who have set their faces towards the heights of Blessed Vision. As we read his words now, he seems to stand and beckon to us, saying, "Come on, my fellow Pilgrims; it is straight ahead to the Shining Gateway; I have blazed the track for you." In sending forth this, another posthumous volume from his pen, we have no doubt but that it will help many and many an aspiring soul up to the heights, until at last they too stand within *The shining Gateway.*

LILY L. ALLEN.
"Bryngoleu," Ilfracombe, ENGLAND

Behold the shining gateway

He who attaineth unto Purity
The faultless Parthenon of Truth doth use
Awake ! Disperse the dreams of self and sin?
Behold the Shining Gateway! Enter in!

1. The shining gateway of meditation

Be watchful, fearless, faithful, patient, pure:
By earnest meditation sound the depths
Profound of life, and scale the heights sublime

Of Love and Wisdom. He who does not find
The Way of Meditation cannot reach
Emancipation and enlightenment.

The unregenerate man is subject to these three things — *Desire, Passion, Sorrow.* He lives habitually in these conditions, and neither questions nor examines them. He regards them as his life itself, and cannot conceive of any life apart from them. To-day he desires, to-morrow he indulges his passions, and the third day he grieves; by these three things (which are always found together) he is impelled, and does not know why he is so impelled; the inner forces of desire and passion arise, almost automatically, within him, and he gratifies their demands *Sans* question; led on blindly by his blind desires, he falls, periodically, into the ditches of remorse and sorrow. His condition is not merely unintelligible to him, it is unperceived: for so immersed is he in the desire (or self) consciousness that he cannot step outside of it, as it were, to examine it.

To such a man the idea of rising above desire and suffering into a new life where such things do not obtain seems ridiculous. He associates all life with *the pleasurable gratification of desire,* and so, by the law of reaction, he also lives in the misery of afflictions, fluctuating ceaselessly between pleasure and pain.

When reflection dawns in the mind, there arises a sense (dim and uncertain at first) of a calmer, wiser, and loftier life; and as the stages of introspection and self-analysis are reached, this sense increases in clearness and intensity, so that by the time the first three stages are fully completed, a conviction of the reality of such a life and of the possibility of attaining it is firmly fixed in the mind.

Such conviction, which consists of a steadfast belief in the supremacy of purity and goodness over desire and passion, is called *faith.* Such faith is the stay, support and comfort of the man who, while yet in the darkness, is searching earnestly for the Light which breaks upon him for the first time in all its dazzling splendour and ineffable majesty when he enters the Shining Gateway of Meditation. Without such faith he could not stand for a single day against the trials, failures, and difficulties which beset him continually, much less could be courageously fight and overcome them, and his final conquest and salvation would be impossible.

Upon entering the stage of meditation, faith gradually ripens into knowledge, and the new regenerate life begins to be realised in its quiet wisdom, calm beauty, and ordered strength, and day by day its joy and splendour increase.

The final conquest over sin is now assured. Lust, hatred, anger, covetousness, pride and vanity, desire for pleasure, wealth, and fame, worldly honour and power –all these have become dead things, shortly to pass away for ever; there is no more life nor happiness in them; they have no part in the life of the regenerate one, who knows that he can never again go back to them, for now the "Old man" of self and sin is dead, and the "new man" of Love and Purity is born within him. He has become (or becomes, as the process of meditation ripens and bears fruit) a new being, one in whom Purity, Love, Wisdom, and Peacefulness are the ruling qualities, and wherein strifes, envies, suspicions, hatreds, and jealousies cannot find lodgment. "Old things have passed away, and, behold, all things have become new"; men and things are seen in a different light, and a new universe is unveiled; there is no confusion; as out of the inner chaos of conflicting desires, passions, and sufferings the new being arises, there arises in the outer world of apparently irreconcilable conditions a new Cosmos, ordered, sequential, harmonious, ineffably glorious, faultless in equity.

Meditation is a process both of *Purification* and *Adjustment.* Aspiration is the purifying element, and the harmonising power resides in the intellectual train of thought involved.

When the stage of meditation is reached and entered upon, two distinct processes of spiritual transmutation is reached and entered upon, two distinct processes of spiritual transmutation begin to take place, namely:

1. Transmutation of passion.
2. Transmutation of affliction.

The two conditions proceed simultaneously, as they are interdependent, and act and react one upon the other.

Passion and affliction, or sin and suffering, are two aspects of one thing, namely, the *Self* in man, that self which is the source of all the troubles which afflict mankind. They represent *Power*, but power wrongly used. Passion is a lower manifestation of a divine energy which possesses a higher use and application. Affliction is the limitation and negation of that energy, and is therefore a means of restoring harmony.

"It says, in effect to the self-bound man, "Thus far shalt thou go and no farther." The man of meditation transfers the passional energy from the realm of evil (Self-following) to the realm, of good (self-overcoming).

To-day he reflects, tomorrow he overcomes his passions, and the third day he rejoices. The mind is drawn from its downward tendency, and is directed upwards. The base metal of error is transmuted into the pure gold of Truth. Lust, hatred, and selfishness disappear; and purity, love, and goodwill take their place.

As the stage proceeds, the mind becomes more and more firmly fixed in the higher manifestations, and it becomes increasingly difficult for it to think and act in the lower; and just in the measure that the mind is freed from the lower, violent, and inharmonious activities, just so much is passion transmuted into power, and affliction into bliss.

This means that there is no such thing as affliction to the sinless man. When sin is put away, affliction disappears.

Selfhood is the source of suffering; Truth is the source of bliss.

When the unregenerate man is abused, or slandered, misunderstood, or persecuted, it causes him intense suffering; but when these things are brought to bear on the regenerate man, there arises in him the rapture of heavenly bliss. None but he who has put away the great enemy, self, under his feet can fully enter into and understand the saying.:

Blessed are ye, when men shall revile you, and persecute you, and shall say all manner of evil against you falsely, for my sake. Rejoice, and be exceeding glad.

And why does the righteous (regenerate) man rejoice under those conditions which cause such misery to the unrighteous (unregenerate) man? It is because, having overcome the evil in himself, he ceases to see evil without. To the good man all things are good, and he utilises everything for the good of the world. To him persecution is not an evil, it is a good.

Having acquired insight, knowledge, and power, he, by meeting that persecution in a loving spirit, helps and uplifts his persecutors, and accelerates their spiritual progress, though they themselves know it not at the time.

Thus he is filled with unspeakable bliss because he has conquered the forces of evil; because, instead of succumbing to those forces, he has learned how to use and direct them for the good and gain of mankind.

He is blessed because he is at one with all men, because he is reconciled to the universe, and has brought himself into harmony with the Cosmic Order.

The following symbol will perhaps help the mind of the reader to more readily grasp what has been explained.

LOVE, LIGHT, AND LIFE
KNOWLEDGE

ASPIRATION, PASSION, AFFLICTION, AND DESIRE

IGNORANCE
LUST, DARKNESS AND DEATH

There is at first the underworld of *lust, darkness,* and *death* which is associated with ignorance; rooted in this is the foot of the cross—*desire*; in the body of the cross, desire branches out into two arms— the right (active or positive) are, *passion,* being equalised and balanced by the left (passive or negative) arm of affliction; uniting these, and rising out of them at the head of the cross, is aspiration; here, wounded and bleeding, rests the thorn-crowned head, of humanity; at the end of this, and right at the summit of the cross, *is knowledge,* which, while being at the apex of the self-life, is the base of the Truth-life; and above rises the heavenly world of *Love, Light,* and *Life.*

In this supremely beautiful world the regenerate man lives, even while living on this earth. He has reached Nirvana, the Kingdom of Heaven. He has taken up his cross, and there is no more sin and sufferings desire and passion and affliction are passed away. Harmony is restored, and all is bliss and peace.

The cross is the symbol of pain. Desire is painful, passion is painful, affliction is painful, and. aspiration is painful; this is why these things are symbolised by a cross which has two pairs of conflicting poles. Affliction is the harmonising and purifying element in passion; aspiration is the harmonising and purifying element in desire. Where the one is, the other must be also. Take away the one, and the other disappears. Suffering, or affliction, is necessary to counteract passion; aspiration, or prayer, is necessary to purge away desire; but for the regenerate man all these things are ended; he has-risen into a new life and a new order of things—the consciousness of purity; lacking nothing and being at one with all things, he does not need to pray for anything; redeemed and reconciled, contented and ill peace, he finds nothing in the universe to hate or fear, and his is both the duty and the power to work without ceasing for the present good and the ultimate salvation of mankind.

2. Temptation

> I know that sorrow follows passion; know
> That grief and emptiness and heartache wait
> Upon all earthly joys; so am I sad;
> Yet Truth must be, and being, can be found;
> And though I am in sorrow, this I know—
> I shall be glad when I have found the Truth.

The only external tempters of man are *The objects of Sensation.* These, however, are powerless *in themselves* until they are reflected in his mind as desirable objects to possess. His only enemy, therefore, is his *coveting of the objects of sensation.* By ceasing to covet objects of sensation, temptation and the painful fighting against impure desires pass away. This ceasing to covet objects of *sensation* is called the *relinquishing of* desire; it is *the renunciation of the inner defilement,* by which a man ceases to be the slave of outward things, and becomes their master.

Temptation is a growth, a process more or less slow, the duration of which can be measured by the sage who has gained accurate knowledge of the nature of his thoughts and acts and the laws governing them, by virtue of having subjected himself to a long course of training in mental discipline and self-control. It has its five stages, which can be clearly defined, and their development traced with precision. But the man who is still immersed in temptation has, as yet, little or no knowledge of the nature of his thoughts and acts and the laws governing them. He has lived so long in outward things—in the objects of sensation—and has given so little time to introspection and the cleansing of his heart, that he lives in almost total ignorance of the real nature of his thoughts and acts which he thinks and commits every day. To him, temptation seems to be instantaneous, and his powerlessness to combat the sudden and, apparently, unaccountable on slaught, causes him to regard it as a *mystery*, and mystery being the mother of superstition, he may and usually does fall back upon some speculative belief to account for his trouble, such as the belief in an invisible Evil

Being, or power, outside himself who suddenly, and without warning, attacks and torments him. Such a superstition renders him more powerless still, for he has sufficient knowledge to understand that he cannot hope to successfully cope with a being more powerful than himself, and of whose whereabouts and tactics he is altogether unacquainted; and so he introduces other beliefs and superstitions which his dilemma seems to necessitate, until at last; in addition to all his sins and sufferings, he becomes burdened with a mass of supernatural beliefs which engross his attention, and take him farther and farther away from the real cause of his difficulty. Meantime he continues to be tempted and to fall, and must do so until by self-subjugation and self-purification he has acquired the ability to trace the relation between cause and effect in his spiritual nature, when, with purified and enlightened vision, he will see that *the moment of temptation is but the fulfilment of those impure desires which he secretly harbours in his own heart.* And, later, with a still purer heart, and when he has gained sufficient control over his wandering thoughts to be able to analyse and understand them, he will see that the *actual moment of temptation itself* has its inception, its growth, and its fruition.

What, then, are the stages in temptation? And how is the process of temptation born in the mind? How does it grow and bear its bitter fruit? The stages are five, and are as follows .

1. PERCEPTION

2. COGITATION

3. CONCEPTION

4. ATTRACTION and

5. DESIRE

The first stage is that in which objects of sensation are *perceived as objects.* This is pure perception, and is without sin or defilement. The second stage is that in which objects of sensation are *considered as objects of personal pleasure.* This is a brooding of the mind upon objects, with an undefined groping for pleasurable sensation, and is the beginning of defilement and sin. In the third stage objects of sensation are *conceived as objects of pleasure.* In this stage the objects are associated with certain pleasurable sensations, and these sensations are conceived and called up vividly in the mind. In the fourth stage objects of sensation are *perceived as objects of pleasure.* At this stage the pleasure as connected with the object is distinctly defined, yet there is a confusion of *pleasure* and *object,* so that the two appear as one, and a wish to possess the object arises in the mind; there is also a going out of the mind towards the object. The fifth and last stage is an intense desire, a coveting and lusting to possess the object in order to experience the pleasure and gratification which it will afford. With every repetition, in the mind, of the first four stages, this desire is added to, as fuel is added to fire, and it increases in intensity and ardour until at last the whole being is aflame with a burning passion which is blind to everything but its own immediate pleasure and gratification. And when this painful fruition of thought is reached, a man is said to be tempted. There is a still further stage of Action, which is merely the doing of the thing desired, the outworking of the sin already committed in the mind. From desire to action is but a short step.

The following table will better enable the mind of the reader to grasp the process and principle involved.

Inaction - Holiness; Rest.

1. Perception. Objects of Sensation *Perceived* as such.
2. Cogitation. Objects of Sensation *Considered* as a source of pleasure.
3. Conception. Objects of Sensation *Conceived* as affording pleasure.
4. Attraction. Objects of Sensation *Perceived* as pleasurable in possession.
5. Desire. Objects of Sensation *Coveted* as such: i.e., desired for personal delight and pleasure.

Action—*Sin; Unrest.*

Every time a man is tempted, he passes, from *inaction,* though all the five stages in succession, and his fall is a passing on into *Action.* The process varies greatly in duration according to the nature of the temptation and the character of the tempted; but after much yielding and many falls, the mind becomes so familiar with the transition that it passes through all the stages with such rapidity as *to* make the temptation appear as an instantaneous, indivisible experience.

The sage, however, never loses sight of the duration of time occupied in the process of temptation, but watches its growth and transition; and just as the scientist can measure the time occupied in the transition of sensation from the brain to the bodily extremities, or from the extremities to the brain, which, ordinarily, appears not to occupy duration, so the sage measures (though by a different method) the passage from pure perception to inflamed desire in a sudden experience of temptation.

This knowledge of the nature of temptation destroys its power, or rather its *apparent* power, for power exists in holiness only. Ignorance is at the root of all sin, and it fades away when knowledge is admitted into the mind. Just as darkness and the effects of darkness disappear when light is introduced, so sin and its effects are dispersed when knowledge of one's spiritual nature is acquired and embraced.

How, then, does the sage avoid sin and remain in peace? Knowing the nature of sinful acts—how they are the result of temptation; knowing also the nature of temptation-how it is the end—and fruition of a particular train of thought, *he cuts off that train of thought at its commencement,* not allowing his mind to go out into the world of sensation, which is the world of pain and sorrow. He stands over his mind,, eternally vigilant, and does not allow his thoughts to pass beyond the safe gates *of pure perception.* To him "all things are pure" because his mind is pure- He sees all objects, whether material or mental, *as they are,* and not as the pleasure-seeker sees them —as objects of personal enjoyment; nor as the tempted one sees them—as sources of evil and pain. His normal sphere, however, is that of *Inaction,* which is perfect holiness and rest. This is a position of entire indifference to considerations of pleasure and pain, regarding all things from the standpoint of *right,* and not from that of *enjoyment.* Is, then, the sage, the sinless one, deprived of all enjoyment? Is his life a dead monotony of inaction—inertia? Truly, he is delivered from all those sensory excitement which the world calls "pleasure", but which conceals, as a mask, the drawn features of pain; and, being released from the bondage of cravings and pleasures, he lives without ceasing in the divine, abiding joy which the pleasure-seeker and the wanderer in sin can neither know nor understand; but *inaction* in this particular means inaction as regards sin; inaction in the lower animal activities which, being cut off, their energy is transferred to the higher intellectual and moral activities, releasing their power, and giving them untrammelled scope and freedom.

Thus the sage avoids sin by extracting its root within himself, not allowing it to grow into attraction, to blossom into desire, and to bear the bitter fruits of sinful actions. The unwise man, however, allows the thought of pleasure to take root in his mind, where its growth, evokes sensations which are pleasant to him, and on these sensations he dwells with enjoyment, thinking in his heart, "So long as I do not commit the sinful act, I am free from sin." He does not know that his thoughts are causes the effects of which are actions, and that there is *no escape from sinful acts for him who dwells in sinful thoughts.* And so the process develops in his mind and blossoms into desire, and in the final moment of temptation (which is but the moment of opportunity brought into prominence by that desire), with the coveted object at his unreserved command, the fall of the man into sinful action is swift and certain.

3. Regeneration

Submit to naught but nobleness; rejoice
Like a strong athlete straining for the prize,
When thy full strength is tried; be not the slave
Of lusts and cravings and indulgences,
Of disappointments, miseries, and griefs,
Fears, doubts, and lamentations, but control
Thyself with calmness; master, that in thee
Which masters others, and which heretofore
Has mastered thee; let not thy passions rule,
But rule thy passions; subjugate thyself Till
passion is transmuted into peace,
And wisdom crown thee; so shalt thou attain
And, by attaining, know.

HAVING considered and examined the nature of temptation in its five interdependent stages, let us now turn to the process of regeneration, and also consider its nature, so that the reader who has already received some measure of enlightenment may be still further guided in his strenuous climbing towards the Perfect Life.

The five stages in regeneration (already enumerated) are:— 1. Reflection; 2. Introspection; 3. Self-analysis; 4. Meditation; and 5. Pure Perception.

The first stage in a pure and true life is that of *thoughtfulness.* The thoughtless cannot enter the right way in life. Only the reflective mind can acquire wisdom. When a man, ceasing to go after enjoyment, brings himself to a standstill in order to examine his position, and to reflect upon the condition of the world and the meaning of life, then he has entered upon the first stage of regeneration. When a man begins to think seriously, and with a deep and noble purpose in view, he has stepped out of the broad way where the thoughtless and the frivolous clutch at the bubbles of pleasure, and has entered the narrow way where the thoughtful and the wise comprehend eternal verities. Such a man's liberation from sin and suffering is already assured; for though he is, as yet, surrounded by much uncertainty, he is already realising a foretaste of the peace which awaits him; his passions, though still strong, are quieter; his mind is calmer and clearer; his intercourse with others is purer and graver; and in his moments of deepest thought he sees, as in a vision, the strength and calmness and wisdom which he knows will one day be his well-earned possessions.

Thus he passes on to the second stage.

Reflecting day by day, with ever-increasing earnestness upon life in all its phases, he comes to perceive the passions and desires in which men are involved, and realises the sorrows which are connected with their strangely ephemeral existence. He sees the burning fevers of lusts and ambitions and cravings for pleasure, and the chilling agues of anxieties and fears, and the uncertainty of slowly approaching death, and he aspires to know the meaning of it all; is eager to find the source and cause of that seems so sorrowful and inexplicable. Recognising himself as a unit in humanity, as one involved in like passions and sorrows with all other men, he vaguely understands that somehow the secret of all life is inevitably bound up with the neophyte, with mind purified, calmed, and his own existence, and so, unsatisfied with the surface theories which are based on observation only, and which still leave him subject to passions and sorrows, and the prey of anxieties and fears, he turns his thoughts inwardly upon his own mind, thinking, perchance, that the wished-for revelation of wisdom and peace awaits him there. Thus he becomes *introspective,* and so he passes on to the third stage.

When the introspective habit is fully ripened and acquired, there is called up in the mind a subtle process of inductive thought by the aid of which the innermost recesses of the man's nature, and, therefore, of all humanity, begin to unveil themselves, and yield up their secrets to the penetrating insight of the patient searcher who, unravelling now the tangled threads of thought, and tracing out the warp and woof of the web of life as it is woven in the mental processes and by the swift-flying shuttle of thought, begins, for the first time, to somewhat clearly comprehend the inner causes of human deeds and the meaning and purpose of existence. As this process of thought is proceeded with, the desires and passions are purified away from the mind; the calmness necessary to a right perception of Truth is acquired; and gradually the fixed principles of things are presented to the comprehension and the eternal laws of life are coherently grasped by the understanding.

And now, quietly, and almost as imperceptibly as the soft light of dawn stealing upon the sleeping world, controlled, passes into the fourth stage, and opens his long-sleeping eyes upon the rising light of Truth. He becomes habitually meditative, and in meditation he finds the master-key which unlocks the Door of Knowledge. It is at this advanced stage in the process of regeneration that the sinner becomes the saint, and the pupil is transformed into the master; for here the process of transmutation, hitherto slow and painful, is greatly accelerated, so that the spiritual forces formerly spent in pleasures, gratifications, passions, and afflictions are now conserved, controlled, and turned into channels of productive and reproductive thought, and so wisdom is born in the mind, and bliss, and peace.

As skill and power are acquired in meditation, the fifth and last stage is reached, where the perfect insight of the seer and the sage is evolved, so that the facts of life are grasped, and the laws and principles of things stand revealed. Here the man is altogether regenerated, is purified and perfected; all human passions are conquered, and human sorrows transcended. Here things are seen *as they are;* all the intricacies of life stand out naked in the light of Truth, and there is no more doubt and perplexity, no more sin and anguish; for he whose pure and enlightened eyes perceive the hidden causes and effects which operate infallibly in human life—he who knows how the bitter fruits of passion ripen, and where the dark waters of sorrow spring—he it is who no more sins and no more sorrows. Lo ! he has come to peace.

The five stages so passed through may be thus presented:

Ignorance—*Sin; Suffering.*

    1. Reflection. Deep and earnest thought on the nature and meaning of life.

2. Introspection. Looking inwardly, for the causes and effects which operate in life.

3. Self-analysis. Searching the springs of thought and purifying the motives in order to find the truth of life.

4. Meditation. Pure and discriminative thought on the facts and principles of life.

5. Pure Perception. Insight. Direct knowledge of the laws of life.

Enlightenment—*Purity; Peace.*

The whole process of regeneration may be likened to the growth of a plant. At first the small seed of *reflection* is cast into the dark soil of ignorance; then the little rootlets come forth and grope about for light and sustenance (introspection); next the strenuous *self-examination* is as the plant reaching upwards toward the light; and then the development of the bud and opening flower of *meditation,* ending at last in that pure and wise *insight* which is the spiritual glory of the sage, the perfect flower of enlightenment.

Thus beginning in sin and suffering, and passing through thoughtfulness, self-searching, self-purification, meditation, and insight, the seeker after the pure life and the divine wisdom reaches at last the undented habitation of a spotless life, and so passes beyond the dark halls of suffering, knowing the perfect Law.

4. Actions and motives

Obey the Right,
And wrong shall ne'er again assail thy peace,
Nor error hurt thee more: attune thy heart
To Purity, and thou shalt reach the
Place Where sorrow is not, and all evil ends.

It has been said that " the way to hell is paved with good intentions," and one frequently hears sin excused on the ground that it was done with a "good motive."

There are actions which are bad-in-themselves, and there are actions which are good-in-themselves, and good intentions cannot make the former good— selfish intentions cannot make the latter bad. Foremost among actions which are bad-in-themselves are those which are classified as "criminal" by all civilised communities. Thus murder, theft, adultery, libel, etc, are always bad, and it is not necessary to inquire into the motive which prompts them. Black and white remain black and white to all eternity, and are not altered by specious argumentations. A lie is eternally a lie, and no number of good intentions can turn it into a truth. If a man tell a lie with a good intention, he has none the less uttered a lie; if a man speak the truth with a selfish intention, he has none the less spoken the truth.

Beside those actions above mentioned, there are others which, while not classified by the law of the land as criminal, are yet recognised as wrong by nearly all intelligent people-actions pertaining to social and family life, and to our everyday relations with our fellowmen. Thus when a child wilfully violates its duty to its parents, the father does not stop to inquire into the motives of the child, but metes out the due correction, because the act of disobedience is *wrong-in-itself.*

The reader may here ask, "In being taught, then, to regard the motive, the condition of heart, as all important, and the act as secondary, have we been taught wrongly?" No, you have not. The *motive is* all important, for it determines the nature of the act, and here we must distinguish between *intentions* and *motives.* When people speak of good and bad motives, they nearly always mean good or bad intentions— that is, the action is done with a certain object, good or bad, in view. The motive is the deeply seated *cause* in the mind, the habitual condition of heart; the intention is the *purpose* in view. Thus an act- may spring from an impure motive, yet be done with the best intention. It is possible for one to be involved in wrong motives, and yet at the same time to be so charged with good intentions as to be continually intruding himself on other people, and interfering in their business and their lives under the delusion that they "need his help."

Intentions are more or less superficial, and are largely matters of impulse, while motives are more deeply seated, and are concerned with a man's fixed moral condition. A man may do an action to-day with a good intention, and in a few weeks' time do the same action with a bad intention; but in both instances the motive underlying the action will be the same.

In reality a wrong act cannot spring from a right motive, although it may be guided by a good intention. A man who can resort, whether habitually or under stress of temptation, to murder, theft, lying or other actions known as bad, is in a dark, confused condition of mind, and is not capable of acting from right motives. Such acts can only spring from an impure source; and this is why the Great Teachers rarely refer to motives , but always refer to actions,. In their precepts they tell us what actions are bad and what are good, without any reference to motive, for the bad and good acts-in-themselves are the fruits of bad and good motives. "By their fruits you shall know them."

In being exhorted to "judge not," we are not taught to persuade ourselves that grapes are figs and figs grapes, but must employ our judgment in clearly distinguishing between the two; so in like manner must we distinguish with unmistakable clearness between bad actions and good actions, so as to avoid the former and embrace the latter; for only in this way can one purify his heart and render himself capable of acting from right motives. A clear perception of what is bad or good, both in ourselves and others, is not false judgment, it is wisdom. It is only when one harbours groundless suspicion about others, and reads into their actions bad and selfish intentions, that he falls into that judging against which we are warned, and which is so pernicious.

There is no need to doubt the good intentions of those about us, while, at the same time, being fully alive to a knowledge of those bad actions which were better left undone, and those good actions which were better done; taking care not to do the former, and to do the latter ourselves, thus teaching by our lives instead of accusing and condemning others. Numberless wrong actions are committed every day with good intentions; and this is why so many good purposes are frustrated and end in disappointment, because the underlying motive is impure, and the good fruit which is sought does not appear; the act is out of harmony with the good intent; the means are not adapted to the end. Bad actions, bring forth bitter fruit; good actions bring forth sweet fruit.

The law runs, "Thou shalt not kill; thou shalt not steal; thou shalt not commit adultery"; not "Thou shalt not kill, steal or commit adultery *with a bad motive.*

Wrong actions are always accompanied with self-delusion, and the chief form which such self-delusion assumes is that of self-justification. If a man flatter himself that he can commit a sinful act, and yet be free from sin because he is prompted by a "pure motive," no limit can be set to the evil which he may commit.

It will be found that bad actions, in the majority of instances, arc accompanied with good intentions. The object of the slanderer generally is to protect his fellow-men from one another. Troubled with foolish suspicions, or smarting under the thought of injury, he warns men against each other, speaking only of their bad qualities, and, in his eagerness, distorting the truth. His intention is good, namely, to protect his neighbours; but his motive is bad, namely, hatred of those whom he slanders. Such a man's good intention is frustrated by his bad action, and he at last only succeeds in separating himself from all truth-loving people.

The sore of a bad action is not cured by plastering it over with good intentions, nor is the cause of the defilement removed from the heart.

Men who are involved in bad actions cannot work from pure motives. An issue of foul water always proceeds from an impure source; and an issue of impure actions proceeds from a heart that is defiled.

It greatly simplifies life, and solves all complex problems of conduct, when certain actions are recognised as eternally bad, and others as eternally good, and the bad are for ever abandoned, and final refuge is taken in the good.

The wise and good perform good actions; and motive, act, and intention being harmoniously adjusted, their lives are powerful for good, and free from disappointment, and the good fruit of their efforts appears in due season. They do not need to defend their actions by subtle and specious arguments, not to enter into interminable metaphysical speculations concerning motives; but are content to act and to leave their actions to bear their own fruit.

Let us not try to persuade ourselves that our good intentions will wipe out the results of our bad actions; but let us resort to the practice of good actions; for only in this way can we acquire goodness; only thus can the life be established on fixed principles, and the mind be rendered capable of comprehending, and working from, pure motives.

5. Morality and religion

The wise man
By adding thought to thought and deed to deed
In ways of good, buildeth his character.
Little by little he accomplishes

His noble ends; in quiet patience works Diligently.
Daily he builds into his heart and mind
Pure thoughts, high aspirations, selfless deeds.
Until at last the edifice of Truth
Is finished, and behold ! there rises and appears
The Temple of Perfection.

There is no surer indication of confusion and decadence in spiritual matters than the severance of morality from religion. "He is a highly moral man, but he is not religious"; "He is exceptionally good and virtuous, but is not at all spiritual," are common expressions on the lips of large numbers of people who thus regard religion as something quite distinct from goodness, purity, and right-living.

If religion be regarded merely and only as worship combined with adherence to a particular form of faith, then it would be correct to say, "He is a very good man, but is not religious," in some instances, just as it would be equally correct to say, "He is an immoral man, but is very religious," in other instances, for murderers, thieves, and other evil-doers are sometimes devout worshippers and zealous adherents to a creed.

Such a narrowing down *of* religion, however, would' render much of the Sermon on the Mount superfluous, from a religious point of view, and would lead to the confounding of the *means* of religion with its *end,* the idolising of the *letter* of religion to the exclusion of the *spirit;* and this is what actually occurs when morality is severed from religion, and is regarded as something alien and distinct from it.

Religion, however, has a broader significance than this, and the most obscure creed embodies in its ritual some longing human cry for that goodness, that virtue, that morality, which many, with thoughtless judgement, divorce from religion. And is not a life of moral excellence, *of good* and noble character, of pure-heartedness, the very end and object of religion? Is it not the substance and spirit, of which worship and adherence to a form of faith are but the shadow and letter?

In religion, as in other things, there are the means and the end, the methods and the attainment. Worship, beliefs about God, adherence to creeds—these are some of the means; goodness, virtue, morality—these are the end. The methods are many and Various, and they are embodied in countless forms of faith; but the end is one—it is moral grandeur !

Thus the moral man, far from being irreligious because he. may not openly profess some form of worship, possesses the substance of religion, diffuses its spirit, has attained its end; and when the sweet Kernel of religion is found and enjoyed, the shell, protective and necessary in its place, has served its purpose, and may be dispensed with.

Let not this, however, be misunderstood. The "moral" man does not refer to one who has only the outward form of morality, appearing moral in the eyes of the world, but keeping his vices secret; nor does it refer to him whose morality extends only to legal limits; nor to those who are proud of their morality—for pride is the reverse of moral—but to those who delight in purity, who are gracious, gentle, unselfish, and thoughtful, who, being good at heart, pour forth the fragrance of pure thoughts and good deeds. By the "moral" is meant the good, the pure, the noble, and the true-hearted.

A man may call himself Christian, Jew, Buddhist, Mohammedan, Hindu—or by any other name—and be immoral; but if one is pure-hearted, if he is true and noble and beautiful in character—in a word, if he is moral—then he is an inhabitant of the "Holy City" in which, there is "no temple"; he is, by example and influence, a regenerator of mankind; he is one of the company of the Children of Light.

6. Memory, repetition, and habit

I shall gain.
By purity and strong self-mastery,
The awakened vision that doth set men free
From painful slumber and the night of grief.

When a particular combination of words has been repeated a number of times, it is said to have been committed to memory— that is, it can then be repeated without visual reference to the words themselves, and without pause or effort; indeed, the words have then a tendency to repeat themselves in the mind, and sometimes people are troubled with the ringing of a refrain, or the repetition of a sentence in the mind, which they find it very difficult to get rid of and forget.

There is a sense in which the whole of life is a process of committing to memory. At first there is *act,* from act springs *experience,* from experience arises *recollection,* from recollection *repetition,* and from repetition is formed *habit*; hence proceeds impulse, faculty, character, individualised existence.

Life is a repetition of the same things over again. There is very little difference between the days and years in the life of a man; one is almost entirely a repetition of the other. Every being is an accumulation of experiences gathered, learnt, and woven into the life by a ceaseless series of repetitions extending over an incalculable number of lives which thread their way through eons of time.

The life of a man, from the germ-cell to maturity, is a repetition, in synthesis, of the entire process of evolution. There is a cosmic memory at the root of all growth and progress, which is an informing and sustaining principle in the process of evolution.

The sensuous memory of man is fickle and ephemeral, but the supersensuous memory which is inherent in all matter, building up forms and faculty is infallible in its reproduction of experiences.

Life is ceaseless reiteration. Nature ever travels over old and familiar ground. Man is daily repeating that which he has learnt though: the schools of experience in which the lessons were acquired may be long forgotten; but the acquired habit is not forgotten; it is carried forward and continues to act. The unconscious and automatic ease which marks the play of faculty is not the ready-made mechanism of an arbitrary creator; it is *skill acquired by practice;* it is the consummation of millions of repetitions of. the same thought and act.

Thoughts and deeds long persisted in become at last spontaneous impulses.

It is a profound truth that "there is nothing new under the sun." It is possible and highly probable that, in the round of eternity, even all our modern inventions and mechanical marvels have been produced innumerable times on this or other worlds. In this world, new combinations of matter appear from time to time, but are they new in the universe? Who dare say that, in the mind which overarches eternity, the cosmic memory is not reproducing things long since fashioned out of itself?

Nothing can be added to, or taken from, the universe. Its matter can neither be increased nor decreased. Chemical combinations of matter vary, but matter itself cannot vary. Life likewise does not change. In the forms of life there is continuous flux, but in the principle of life there is no increase or diminution. Forms come forth only to retreat and disappear; but that which disappears is not lost; the memory of it is retained, and it continues to be repeated. Eternal disintegration is balanced by eternal restitution.

The mind of man is not separate from the Eternal Mind; in its daily repetitions is indelibly written the record of all its past. *Character is an accumulation of deeds.* Each man is the last reckoning in the long sum of evolution, and there is no falsification of the account. The mind continues to automatically perform the habit which encloses a million repetitions of the same deed. Compared with this ineffaceable, unconscious memory, the memory of three score years and ten is as a fading vapour to an Egyptian Pyramid. The tendencies, impulses, and habits of which a man is a victim are the repetitions of his accumulated deeds. They enfold the destiny which he has wrought. The grace, goodness, and genius which a man exhibits without conscious effort are the fruits of the accumulated labours of his mind. He repeats with ease that which was learned by painful labour. The wise man sees a reflection of himself in the fate which overtakes him.

Life flows in channels. Every man is in a rut. Men tell their fellows to "get out of their ruts," but they themselves are in ruts of another kind. The flow of law, of nature, cannot be avoided, but it can be utilised. We cannot avoid ruts, but we can avoid bad ones; we can follow along good ones.

In their training and education, the children of to-day are strictly confined to ways which are worn by the feet of a thousand generations. In his fixed habits and characteristics, the man of to-day is reviving the actions of a thousand lives.

It is true that men are bound; but it is equally true that they can unbind. The law by which a man becomes the sorrowful victim of his own wrong deeds is a blessed, and not a cursed, law; for by the same law he can become the instrument of all that is good. Habits chain a man, but he himself forged the links. He whose inner eye has opened to perceive the law does not complain. The bondage of evil is a heavy slavery, but the bondage of good is a blessed service.

The will of man is powerless to alter the law of life, but it is powerful to obey it. The Great Law makes for good; it puts a heavy penalty on evil. Man can break his chains, and shake himself free; and when he enters earnestly upon the work of self-liberation, all the universe will be with him in his labour. Repetition and habit he cannot avoid, but he can set going repetitions that are harmonious, he can form habits that will crystallise into pure and noble characteristics.

In the self-built archives of the mind are stored away the entire records of man's evolution. Man is an epitomised history of the world. In his outbursts of rage we hear again the roar of the lion in the forest; in his selfish schemings to secure his coveted ends we see the tiger stalking its prey; his lusts, revenges, hatreds, and fears are the instinct born of primeval experiences. The universe does not forget; life remembers and restores.

Between the sensuous and the supersensuous worlds is the Lethean stream, the river of forgetfulness. Only he who has passed into the supersensuous world—the world of pure goodness—remembers with the Memory of Life which transcends a million deaths. Only he whose will obeys the Universal Will, whose heart is in harmony with the Cosmic Order, receives the vision which pierces through the vale of time and matter, and sees the before and the beyond.

Man quickly forgets, and it is well that he forgets; the universe remembers and records. The repetition of an evil deed is its own retribution; the repetition of a good deed is its own reward. The deepest punishment of evil is evil; the highest reward of good is good. When a deed is done, it is not ended; it is but begun; it remains with the doer—to curse him, if evil; to bless him, if good. Deeds accumulate by repetition, and they remain as character, and in character is both curse and blessing.

Suffering inheres in the discordant repetition of evil; bliss inheres in the rhythmic repetitions of good. Seeing that we cannot escape the law of repetition, let us choose to do those things which are good; and as one establishes habits of purity, the divine memory will be awakened within him.

7. Words and wisdom

I would find
Where Wisdom is, where Peace abides, where Truth,
Majestic, changeless, and eternal, stands
Untouched by the illusions of the world;

For surely there is Knowledge, Truth, and Peace
For him who seeks.

Thoughts, words, acts—these combine to make up the entire life of every individual. Words and acts are thoughts expressed. We think in words. In the process of thinking, words are stored up in the consciousness, where they await expression and use as occasion may call them forth.

Words fit the mind which received them; they are the tally of the intellect which uses them. The meaner the mind, the more meagre is the vocabulary. A limited and a capacious intellect alike expresses itself through a limited and an extensive use of words. A great mind expresses itself by the vehicle of flowing and noble language.

Words stand for conceptions. Conceptions are embodied in words. At the moment that a conception is formed in the mind, its corresponding word arises in the thought. Conceptions and words cannot be hidden away indefinitely. Sooner or later they will come forth into the outer world of expression. The matter of the universe is in ceaseless circulation. Its hidden things are continuously coming forth into open and visible life. Likewise the mental operations of men are ever in active circulation, and their hidden thoughts are daily expressing themselves in words and acts. The words and actions of every man are determined by the thoughts in which he habitually dwells.

Speech is audible thought. A man reveals him. self through his speech. Whether he is pure or impure, foolish or vice, he makes his inner condition known through his speech. The foolish man is known by the way in which he talks; the wise man is known by the purity, gravity, and excellence of his speech. "He who would gain a knowledge of men." says Confucius, "must first learn to understand the meaning of words "

All wise men, saints, and great teachers have declared that the first step in wisdom is to control the tongue. The disciple of speech is a mental disciple. When a man controls his tongue, he controls his mind; when he purifies his speech, he purifies his mind. Speech and mind cannot be separated. They are two aspects of character.

A man may read Scripture, study religions, and practise mystical arts; but if he allows his tongue to run loosely, he will be as foolish at the end of all his labours as he was at the beginning.

A man may not read Scripture, nor study religions, nor practise ascetic arts; but if he controls his tongue, and studies how to speak wisely and well, he will become wise.

Wisdom is perceived in the words which are its expression. We speak of certain men—of Shakespeare for instance—as being wise. We never saw Shakespeare, and we know very little of his life; how, then, do we know he was wise? By his words only. Where there are wise words, we know there is a wise mind. A foolish man may, like a parrot, *repeat* wise words, but a wise man *frames* wise sentences; his wisdom is shown in originally expressed language.

Why do men speak of words as being bad or good, degrading or inspiring, low or lofty, weak or strong? Is it not because they, unconsciously recognise that words cannot be dissociated from thoughts? Why do pure-minded people avoid a man who habitually uses impure language? Is is not because they know that such words proceed from an unclean mind?

It is impossible for any being to give utterance to words which are not already lodged in his mind fit the form of thought. The impure mind cannot speak pure words; the pure mind cannot speak impure words. The ignorant cannot speak learnedly, nor the learned ignorantly. The foolish man cannot speak wisely, nor the wise foolishly.

Altered speech follows an altered mind. When a man turns from evil to good, his conversation becomes cleansed. As a man increases in wisdom, he watches, modifies, and perfects his speech.

If the foolish and the wise are known by their words, what, then, is the speech of folly, and what the language of wisdom?

A man is foolish:

If he talks aimlessly and incoherently. If he engages in impure conversations. If he utters falsehood. If he speaks ill of the absent, and carries about
evil reports concerning others.
If he frames flattering words.
If he utters violent and abusive words.
If his speech is irreverent, and
his words are directed against the great and good.
If he speaks in praise of himself.

A man is wise:

If he talks with purpose and intelligence.
If his conversation is chaste.
If he utters words of sincerity and truth.
If he speaks well of and in defence of, the absent.
If he speaks words of virtuous reproof.
If his speech is gentle and kindly.
If he talks reverently of the great and good.
If he speaks in praise of others.

We are all, now and always, justified and condemned by our words. The law of Truth is not held in abeyance, and every day is judgement day. For "every idle word" which one speaks he is at once "called to account" in an immediate and certain loss of happiness and influence. By the words which we habitually utter we publish to the universe the degrsee of our intelligence and the standard of our morality, and receive back through them the judgement of the world. The fool thinks he is harshly judged and badly treated by others, not knowing that his real scourge is his own ungoverned tongue.

To control the tongue, to discipline the speech, to strive for the use of purer and gentler words—this is a very lowly thing, and one that is much despised; but it cannot be neglected by him who eagerly aspires to walk the way of wisdom.

8. Truth made manifest

Upon the lofty Summits of the Truth
Where clouds and darkness are not, and where rests
Eternal Splendour; there, abiding Joy
Awaits thy coming.
Be watchful, fearless, faithful, patient, pure:
By earnest meditation sound the depths
Profound of life, and scale the heights sublime
Of Love and Wisdom.

Truth is rendered visible through the media of deeds. It is something seen and not heard. Words do not contain the Truth; they only symbolise it. Good deeds are the only vessels which contain Truth.

It has been frequently said that *being* must precede *doing.* Being always does precede doing; but being; and doing cannot be arbitrarily separated. A man's deeds are the expression of himself. Acts are the language of Reality. If a man's inner being is allied to Truth, his deeds will speak it forth; if with error, his deeds will make manifest that error.

No man can hide what he is. He must necessarily act, and every time he acts he reveals himself.

In the light of Reality no man can deceive humanity or the universe; but he can deceive himself.

Deeds of purity, love, gentleness, patience, humility, compassion, and wisdom are Truth made manifest. These qualities cannot be contained between the covers of a book, but only the words which refer to them; they are Life.

Deeds of impurity, hatred, anger, pride, vanity, and folly are error making itself known. A man's deeds are the publication of himself to the world.

Truth cannot be comprehended through reading, but only by correcting and converting one's self. Precepts are aids to the acquirement of wisdom, but wisdom is acquired only by practice.

If a man would know what measure of Truth he possesses, he should ask himself, "What am I? What are my deeds?"

Men dispute about words, thinking that Truth is heard and read. Truth is neither heard nor read; it is *seen.*

Good deeds are the visible embodiments of Truth; they are messengers of Knowledge; angels of Wisdom; but the eye of error is dark, and cannot see them.

9. Spiritual humility

Who would be the companion of the wise,
And know the Cosmic Splendour; he must stoop
Who seeks to stand; must fall who fain would rise;
Must know the low, ascending to the high;
He who would know the Great must not disdain
To diligently wait upon the small;
He wisdom finds who finds humility,

Throughout the Sacred Scriptures of all religions there runs, like a silver thread, the teaching of Humility. Not only all the Scriptures, but the sages of all time have declared that only through the portal of humility is it possible for man to enter into the possession of the Life of Truth; and as that life is entirely of a spiritual Nature, so the humility that leads to it is purely and absolutely spiritual; and being such, it can never be materialised, can never be embodied in a dogma, or laid down as a formula. It is not an outward thing, nor does it consist of that practice of self-abasement that has usurped its name.

But priests have taught, and many have been led to believe, that self-depreciation is true humility, while in reality it is its extreme antithesis. Self-depreciation is self-degradation; may, it is even a sort of self-destruction, it is spiritual suicide. The man who believes that all his righteousness is as filthy rags, that there is no good thing in him, and that he can never rise by any effort of his own, is by that very attitude of his mind, rendering himself impotent; he is strangling the Spirit; he is undermining and disintegrating all that is highest and noblest in his character. Instead of building up his character he is engaged in despoiling it. "As a man thinketh in his heart, so is he"; what our thoughts are, such are our characters. We are in reality beings composed of thoughts; thoughts are the bricks which we are continually laying down in the building of our souls. If we put a large percentage of rotten bricks into the building, we shall build but a miserable hovel, and every self-depreciating thought is a brick that is already crumbling. It will be found to be a rule marvellously accurate in its application that those who continually live in this attitude of self-depreciation are throughout life, or, at any rate, until they strike a nobler attitude, wretched failures. I can bring to my mind many such men that I have known. How can it be otherwise? How can a man who has no faith in himself ever win the confidence of others, or accomplish anything worthy? Moreover such a man has not, cannot possibly have, any faith in human nature; despising himself, he despises all; and as a result, by the unerring law of cause and effect, all men despise him. Yet it is a strange fact that the men who maintain this faith-destroying attitude of mind invariably profess to have the greatest faith in God; yea, look upon it as an infallible witness to their superior spiritual faith. But I ask this question, Does not true faith, like true charity, begin at home? In the growth of the soul faith in one's self comes first, next faith in human nature, and finally faith in God. That faith which professes to have the latter to the exclusion of the two former is false faith, the outcome of fake humility.

Another kind of false humility is that of *personal abasement* to an individual or to established authority. This is humility materialised or subverted. It is the worship of Dagon, the bowing of the knee to Baal, the slavish adoration of the Golden Calf. No man can persist in it without undermining his character, and ultimately dissipating his spiritual and mental energies. Humility to man or to any temporal authority is degrading and slavish; humility to the Most High is grandly beautiful.

Spiritual humility is closely allied to faith, and the more there is of humility the more there is of faith. It is the key-note of all real greatness. In proof of this I have only to refer to the great sages, saints, and reformers of all time. The greatest of them are those who had the greatest share of spiritual humility. True humility, as distinguished from false, has a strengthening power, an upbuilding force. It inspires and invigorates the soul, spurring is to greater and ever greater endeavour.

Of what, then, does this humility consist? Is it the bending of the knee to ask personal favours of Deity? Is it the blind petitioning of God to accomplish for us our petty and narrow designs? Nay, these are its counterfeits. True humility is far above and. beyond all this. It is the deepest and holiest aspiration of the human heart, where deep within, hidden from all sacrilegious gaze, it works, a silent mighty power, purifying, transforming, the man of flesh and self; entering its solitary grandeur, the alienated soul returns to the foot-stool of its God, and bathes, in blissful rapture, in the light of His all-embracing Love. It is a state that can only be entered into by rising above one's *lower self.* It is in fact the submergence of the self in the *non-self;* the submission of passion and intellect to the Supreme; it is the attitude of a human soul adoring its highest conception.

Such humility takes its possessor above all that is mean and poor in his nature, into the very presence of God, making him calm, strong, noble, self-reliant, and Godlike. It is the Wine of Life to all aspiring souls. The soul that has not felt its power is dead.

It may sound like a paradox, but it is nevertheless true, that the more a man has of humility the more he has of *independence.* But the seeming paradox will be made clear if we think for a moment of the lives of such teachers of humility as Jesus, Buddha, Confucius, Socrates, Jacob Boehme, George Fox, and indeed of all the great religious reformers. These men walked erect, because, yielding themselves up to the simplicity' of humility, they walked with God.

The humility that causes a man to go, metaphorically speaking, on all fours is spurious, and is as debasing and destructive as the real humility is elevating and strengthening.

Why should we go amongst our fellows like cringing, fearful beasts, calling ourselves miserable sinners? Shall we ever rise above sin by so doing? Is it possible to rise by ceaselessly contemplating our absolute unworthiness? No, we can only rise by continually contemplating the Highest. There may be much that is unworthy in a man's heart, but there is also a sacredness, a dignity, a divinity about it; let us dwell upon that. Let us continually contemplate the goodness, the purity, and the essential beauty of human nature, Let us ceaselessly search for the Divinity in our own souls, and, finding it through the door of humility, we shall then recognise the invisible God in all men. By so doing, we rise above the binding limitations of our selfish desires, and enter the larger, healthier, holier life of Love.

10. Spiritual strength

> All things are holy to the holy mind,
> All uses are legitimate and pure,
> All occupations blest and sanctified,
> And every day a Sabbath.

A clear and firm head must precede and accompany a clean and gentle heart. Without the first the second is impossible, for the qualities of purity and gentleness can only be reached through a clear perception of right and wrong, and by the exercise of an irresistible will. The strength of a powerful animal, or of that animal force in man which enables him to gain the victory over others by attack and resistance, is weakness compared with that quiet, patient, invincible will by which a man overcomes himself, and tames to obedience, and trains to the service of holy purposes, the savage passions of his nature.

Every dog can bark and fight, and every foolish man can rail, abuse, fence with hard words, and give way to fits of bad temper; these things are easy and natural to him, and require no effort and no strength. But the wise man puts away all such follies, and trains himself in self-control—trains himself to act unerringly from fixed principles, and not from the fleeting impulses of an unstable nature.

He who succeeds in so training himself is able to train others, in a small degree by precept, but largely and chiefly by practice or example, for it is pre-eminently the prerogative of the wise to teach by their actions. The mockeries of Herod, the accusations of tie people, and the fanatical persecutions of the priests all failed to draw from Jesus the word of complaint, bitterness, or self-defence. Such sublime acts of silence and self-control continue to reach, for ages, both individuals and nations, with far greater power and effect than all the words and books uttered and written by the world's vast army of priests and learned commentators.

To retaliate and fight belongs to the animal in man as it belongs to the beast of the forest; but to refuse to be swayed from the practice of a divine principle by any external pressure—to stand firm and unalterable in goodness and truth alike amid blame and praise—this belongs to the divine in man and in the universe.

To alter one's conduct in order to please others, or to avoid their censure or misunderstanding can never lead to spiritual strength.

That divine kindness which always accompanies spiritual understanding and strength is something very different from merely saying pleasant words—for pleasant words are not always true words—but consist in doing *what is best for the eternal welfare of the other person or persons.*

The weak father, who is unfit to train children only considers how he can escape trouble with his children, and so he slurs over their acts of disobedience and selfishness, and tries to please them. But the strong father, who considers the future character and welfare of his children, knows how and when to administer a severe reproof; fully understanding that the few minutes' pain caused by his rebuke may save his child from years of suffering as a result of loose living which is fostered by parental neglect. The strong, kind, unselfish father, whose care is for his children's good, and not for his own immediate comfort, knows not only how to be tender in affection, but *tender in discipline,* knows how to stretch out the strong and (to the child at the time) severe arm of restraint to save his little ones when they would ignorantly wander away in wrong paths.

So the man of spiritual strength cannot be merely a weak framer of smooth words, but a doer of right actions, an utterer of words that are vital and true, and, therefore, eternally kind.

The spiritually weak man shrinks from right when it is brought (as by its nature it must be brought) in opposition to his desires, and he embraces sin because it is pleasant. The spiritually strong man shrinks from sin, more especially when it is presented to him in a pleasant garb, and embraces right, even though by so doing he will bring upon himself the odium of those who are ignorant of divine principles and their beneficent application.

The man of spiritual understanding is as unbending as a bar of steel where right is concerned, knowing that right alone is good; he is as unresisting as water where self is concerned, knowing that self alone is evil. Acting from imperishable principles and not from the fleeting desires of self, his actions partake of the imperishable nature of the principles from which they spring, and continue to afford instruction and inspiration through unnumbered generations.

It is always the portion of one who so acts to be misunderstood. The majority live in their desires and impulses, following them blindly as they are brought into operation by external stimuli, and do not understand what is meant by acting dispassionately from right and fixed principles, with entire freedom from self interest. Such will necessarily misunderstand and misjudge the right-doer, regarding him as cold and cruel in his unbending adherence to right, or as weak, cowardly in his quiet refusal to passionately defend himself. He will, therefore, "be accused of many things", but this will not cause him any suffering, nor will he be troubled or disturbed thereby, for the truth which he practises is a source of perpetual joy, and he will be at rest in the knowledge that there are those who will understand and follow,' that he is working for the ultimate good even of his accusers; and that by manifesting the truth in his daily actions, he is in the company of those divinely strong ones who are leading the world into ways of quietness and peace.

Poems Of Peace

Eolaus
A lyrical dramatic poem

Dramatis Personae
Eolaus.
The Prophet.
Earth.
Heaven.
Cosmos.
Voices of Nature.
Voices of Truth.
Echoes.

Scene: — *A beautiful Island, wooded.* Eolaus *sitting on a fallen tree near the sea-shore.*

Eolaus. Unto this lonely Island I repair
To search for peace. After long, days and nights
Upon the waters, storm-tossed and fatigued,
My skiff Touched thy fair harbour, blessed Isle.
Now on thy fragrant bosom I will rest,
And in thy spiritual ecstasy
Sweetly participate: thy loveliness
Entrances me; thy restfulness enweaves
My thoughts with peace imperishable; thou
Art silent, solitary, beautiful,
And I am lonely; yet thy solitude
Perchance will comfort me, and take away
My loneliness and pain. O Solitude !
Thou habitation of aspiring hearts;
Thou light and beacon of the pure; thou guide

Of them that cry in darkness; thou sweet friend
Of sorrow stricken wanderers; thou staff
And stay of the strong climber up the hills,
Trackless and strange, of Truth; instructor thou,
And teacher of the teachable and true,

Beloved of the lowly, wise and good,
Be my companion now, and take away
The world's ache from my bosom! I am tired
Of the vain Highways, where the noise and din
Drowns all but sad remembrance; tired of all
The tumult and the terror and the tears
That rule discordant in the House of Life,
Shaking but not destroying, as the storms,
Confederate with the oceans, shake the shores
And rock-bound margins of the continents.
I seek the peace that does not change; the calm
That knows no storm; the Silence that remains.
Pleasure disturbs, and does not satisfy:
When the excitements of the senses fade,
Sorrow and pain return, and leave the heart
Remorseful, desolate. As o'er the waste
And barren moor the lonely curlew cries.
So wails the bird of anguish o'er the mind
Sated with pleasure; Woe and Want repair
To the abode of Selfishness, and take
Legions of miseries with them. I would find
Where Wisdom is, where Peace abides, where Truth,
Majestic, Changeless, and eternal, stands
Untouched by the illusions of the world:
For surely there is Knowledge, Truth, and Peace
For him who seeks, seeing that ignorance
And error and affliction are; these prove
The unseen truths obversely: darkness makes
Light sure and certain, though we see it not.
We sleep and wake, and, waking, know the dream
That troubled us in sleep; how it arose,
Phantasmal and chaotic, in the mind
Left all ungoverned; even so perchance
This life of passion and of wild desire
(Troubled, chaotic, and not understood),
May be, as 'twere, a dream; and if a dream
Of the unmastered mind, we shall awake
Out of the nightmare of our miseries,
And know the gladness of Reality.
But how shall one awake? How, if not by
Bridling his passions, curbing his desires
By masterful dominion of the will?

If passions be the troubled dreams of life,
And not its substance and reality,
Then he who shakes off passion shall awake
And know the Truth; surely this must be so !
Therefore unto this unfrequented place
Have I addressed myself, that I may gain,
By purity and strong self-mastery,
Th' awakened vision that doth set men free
From painful slumber and the night of grief.
Here unobserved and solitary, I
Will purify my heart and train my mind
In the true ways of sweet unselfishness,
Subduing self and passion; so perchance
The changeless Truth will be revealed to me,
And I shall move, wherever Duty calls,
Serene and sorrowless.

Moreover, here
An aged Prophet dwells, so I am told,
Who will instruct me in the Silent Way
Which winds through the morasses of the mind
Unto the firm heights of accomplished Truth.
Him will I seek when I have slept awhile,
For weariness now urges me to rest.

Lies down.

Thou Zephyrus! thou sweet and cooling breath
That temperest the broiling mid-day rays
Of June's extremest heat, blow o'er me now,
And fan me into sweet forgetfulness !
I am a-wearied, battling with the waves.
Now will I sleep: after my long, long search
Upon the waters, I am spent with toil.
Watch o'er me. Nature, I am safe with thee.

Sleeps.

Voices of Nature.

First Voice.

Listen, O Eolaus !

Woven of passion is the Universe;
Vain is thy puny strength to break its web.

Submit thyself to that which in thee cries;
Gratify nature; do not fly delight.
Eolaus, come !
Let me lead thee, Eolaus!
Let me guide thee, Eolaus!
Come, Eolaus! Eolaus, come!

Echo.

Eolaus, come !

Second Voice.

There is sweet intoxication
 In the Pleasure - house of Earth;
Aye - renewed exhilaration,
 Love and happiness and mirth.

First Voice.

Come, Eolaus! Eolaus, come !

Echo.

Eolaus, come !

Third Voice.

What is seen is sure;
What is felt is known
Pleasure is secure;
Joy is life alone.

First Voice.

Come, Eolaus ! Eolaus, come!

Echo.

Eolaus, come!

Second Voice.

Come and drink the wine of life;
Pleasure's vintage come and taste;
Leave thy fruitless search and strife;
Holy vigils wear and waste
Youth, for love and revels framed:
Nature thus is blindly blamed.

First Voice.

Come, Eolaus ! Eolaus, come !

Echo.

Eolaus, come !

Third Voice.

Think no more of low and high;
Leave thy climbings, and forget
Aim and struggle, doubt and sigh;
Level is the pathway set
Of enjoyment: seek no more;
Rest thou here, thy woe is o'er

First Voice.

Eolaus come!
Let me lead thee, Eolaus !
Let me guide thee, Eolaus !
Come, Eolaus! Eolaus, come!

Echo.

Eolaus, come !

Earth.
Unnumbered ages have I rolled
Through the abysmal spaces;
And eons new from eons old
Th' Eternal Finger traces;
And I must follow where it moves;
 No rest ! no rest!
With hopes and fears and hates and loves
Unblest ! unblest!

Fourth Voice.

Listen, O Eolaus !

Sorrow doth darken all the universe;
Its creatures are involved in pain and woe;
Helpless they cry, and no one hears or aids;
Dark, dark is life, and none its meaning know.

Eolaus, hear !
None can lead thee, Eolaus !
None can guide thee, Eolaus !

Hear, Eolaus! Eolaus, hear!

Echo.

Eolaus, hear!

Fifth Voice.

There is pain and woe and sorrow
In the hospital of Earth;
Every night and morn and morrow
Bringeth drought and death and dearth.

Fourth Voice.

Hear, Eolaus ! Eolaus, hear !

Echo.

Eolaus, hear!

Sixth Voice.

What is Sean's unsure;
What is felt is blown;
Self is insecure;
Life is pain alone.

Fourth Voice.

Hear, Eolaus ! Eolaus, hear !

Echo.

Eolaus, hear !

Several Voices.

We moan and sigh;
We sob and cry;
We wander, like the wind upon the stream,
Vainly for peace,
Seeking release
From the keen pain of our unending dream.

Fourth Voice.

Eolaus, hear!
None can lead thee, Eolaus !
one can guide thee, Eolaus !
Hear, Eolaus ! Eolaus, hear!

Echo.

Eolaus, hear!
Voices of Truth.

First Voice.

Awake, O Eolaus!
Arise ! Shake off the dreams of Night,
Open thine eyes, and sec the Light;
Passionless Wisdom waits for thee
In sorrowless serenity.
Leave thou the fleeting shapes of Time,
The rugged Way of Truth sublime
Walk thou; nor fear, nor grieve, nor lust,
Scorning the self whose end is dust.
Wake, Eolaus! Eolaus, wake !

Chorus of Voices.

Eolaus, wake!

Second Voice.

Knowledge is for him who seeks;
Wisdom crowneth him who strives;
Peace in sinless silence speaks;
All things perish, Truth survives

First Voice.

Wake, Eolaus ! Eolaus, wake !

Voices.

Eolaus, wake!

Third Voice.

Follow where Virtue leads,
High and still higher;
Listen when Pureness pleads,
Quench not her fire.
Lo ! he shall see

Reality,
Who cometh upward, cleansed from all desire.

First Voice.

Wake, Eolaus ! Eolaus, wake !

Voices.

Eolaus, wake!

Fourth Voice.

He who attaineth unto Purity
The faultless Parthenon of Truth doth see.
Awake! disperse the dreams of self and sin !
Behold the Shining Gateway ! enter in!

First Voice.

Wake, Eolaus ! Eolaus, wake !

Voices.

Eolaus, wake !

Fifth Voice.

Conquer thyself,
Then thou shalt know;
Climb to the high,
Leave thou the low.
Deliverance
Shall him entrance
Who strives with sins and sorrows, tears and pains
Till he attains.

First Voice.

Wake, Eolaus ! Eolaus, wake !

Voices.

Eolaus, wake!

Heaven.

In the visions of the ages
I am evermore reflected;
In the precepts of the Sages
I am spoken and rejected.

I can suffer no distortion,
Sin and sorrow cannot stain me;
Fixed and faultless in proportion,
He must bend who would attain me.

Eolaus, *waking.*

Who will lead me, who will guide me
In my deep perplexity?

Heaven.

In the middle of the Island
Waits the sage whom you are seeking;
On the Rock which cannot crumble
Sits the Prophet who will guide you.

Eolaus wakes.

Eolaus. 'Mid the conflicting visions of the mind
I darkly grope, and nevermore can find
The steadfastness and surety that I seek;
Where clamour reigns the Silence cannot speak;
So many voices and so many ways !
So many wand'rings the nights and days!
One way I seek, one voice I long to hear,
But Truth eludes me and does not appear,
Now to this Island's centre I repair
To seek the Prophet who abideth there.
*The scene changes to the centre of the Island. An aged and
venerable man appears, sitting upon a rock.*

Eolaus. Art thou the Prophet whom I seek?

Prophet. I am.

Eolaus. Be thou my guide, for thou art wise, and I
Am ignorant; speak thou, and I will hear;
Teach me, and I will be instructed; make
Me to behold the Path which leads to Truth,
And I will walk if though it be o'erstrewn
With flints and burrs; and if it needs must come
Within the round of holy discipline
That one shall walk that way with naked feet,
Or else forego the end and view of Truth,
Then barefoot I will walk it, and account

Bleedings and wounds and lacerations
As aids unto my will and fortitude,
As tasks wisely ordained, and so to be
Gladly encountered in my pilgrimage.
Mine ears are open, open thou mine eyes,
For I am blind, and cannot find my way.

Prophet. He who would see with the all-seeing eye
Single of Truth, must first his blindness know.
He cannot see who does not wish to see,
Thinking he sees already, while his acts
Proclaim his spiritual blindness. Truth
Waits on the Lowly - hearted. He who knows
That being passion - bound, he yet is blind,
Has groped his way to Wisdom. Thou dost see.

Eolaus. I see naught but the darkness of my mind,
And in that darkness ever - changing shapes
Of things phantasmal that perplex and haunt,
Eluding knowledge; I am ignorant,
Yet strive to know; nor will I cease to strive
Till I attain.

Prophet. Seeing thy darkness, thou
So far dost see; knowing thine ignorance,
So far hast thou attained to knowledge: seek,
And thou shalt surely find.

Eolaus. How shall I seek?

Prophet. Increase thy strength and self-reliance; make
The spectres of thy mind obey thy will:
See thou command thyself; nor let no mood,
No subtle passion nor so swift desire
Hurl thee to baseness; but, should'st thou be hurled,
Rise and regain thy manhood, taking gain
Of lowliness and wisdom from thy fall.
Strive ever for the mastery of thy mind,
And glean some good from every circumstance
That shall confront thee; make thy store of strength
Richer for ills encountered and o'ercome.
Submit to naught but nobleness; rejoice
Like a strong athlete straining for the prize,
When thy full strength is tried; be not the slave

Of lusts and cravings and indulgences,
Of disappointments, miseries and griefs,
Fears, doubts, and lamentations, but control
Thyself with calmness; master that in thee:
Which masters others, and which heretofore
Has mastered thee: let not thy passions rule,
But rule thy passions; subjugate thyself
Till passion is transmuted into peace,
And wisdom crown thee; so shalt thou attain
And, by attaining, know.

Eolaus. Hard is the path.
Which thou hast set before me; steep and strange
Its ascent; unfamiliar and unknown
The Place whereto it leads: I see it rise
Precipitous but yet accessible,
Beyond the reach of vision: what awaits
The climber, none but he who climbs may know;
For if one ask, and, with believing ears
Attend the spiritual Mountaineer
In his depicture of the unknown heights,
What knows he more, though more believing? What
Gains he but words, and wonderings, and dreams,
Unless he also climb? I would o'ermount
Faith, and ascend to knowledge; I would not
Rest idly in the valleys of belief,
Content with speculation; I would be
The Mountaineer, and know.

Prophet. The Mountaineer
Is he who, dauntless, climbs.

Eolaus. But yet the way,—
Where leads it? All beyond the reach of sight
Is dark, unknown, mysterious. What avails
The strenuous ascent, if some precipice
The daring climber claim, or loosened rock
Dash him to death, or cold and hunger make
Ravage upon his strength? Passion is sweet,
And 'tis enjoyed and known; and round about
The habitations at the mountain's base,
In the familiar valleys of the mind,
Twine the sweet flowers of soft affections,

Filling the air with fragrance and delight,
And mellow fruits of love and labour hang
Ripe for the plucking; shall I these renounce,
The sure and known, for the unsure, unknown?
Are these not safe, substantial and possessed?
While that I seek,—Where is it? Is this Truth,
This idea of Reality which haunts
My mind, and drives me whither I know not,
Itself a speculation? What abides?
Alas! all that we have and know is caught
In transiency; changes that never end
Roll wave - like o'er the restless universe
.And man is tossed therein; so it befalls
That everything which comes into his grasp—
Bearing the face of an enduring joy—
After a little fever of delight

All things are dying even while they live;
And life is passing while it seems to wait.
There is no sweet possession, no rare joy,
No cherished circumstance, no prized delight
No lovely thing, of which it can be said,—
"There is no time when this will never be."
What comes to pass, passes, and conies no more;
What grows, decays; what rises, falls; what lives
And flourishes, dies and doth fade away:
Where then is surety; Where is knowledge? Where
Is rest and refuge?

Prophet. There is rest in Truth.

Eolaus. Is there no rest in death?

Prophet. There is no rest
In death.

Eolaus. No rest in death nor life?

Prophet. No rest
In death nor life; yet or in death or life,
Where Truth is, there is rest.

Eolaus. Prophet of Good
Lead me to the Abiding; set my feet
Upon the austere Highway which doth lead

To the Eternal City; I would find
The rest and refuge of undying Truth.

Prophet. Look thou within. Lo, in the midst of change
Abides the Changeless; at the heart of strife
The Perfect Peace reposes. At the root
Of all the restless striving of the world
Is passion, and at passion's heart is stored
Truth; yea, the Law of laws is in thy mind,
And written on the tablet of thy heart
Are its eternal edicts: subjugate
Thy passions, and the truth will be revealed,
For whoso follows passion findeth pain,
But whoso conquers passion findeth peace.

Eolaus. Not to be subject unto passion, but
To subject passion,—is this then the way?

Prophet. Thou hast well said. As the sweet nut is held.
In the hard shell, and cannot be enjoyed
But by destruction of the husk, so Truth
In passion is preserved, but is not known
Till passion be destroyed and cast away.
He who preserveth passion, dreading loss
Of sweetness and enjoyment, cannot know
The bliss of Truth, nor find where wisdom is:
He is a prodigal, feeding upon
The husks of life, the empty shows of things.
And knowing not its kernel, seeing not
The changeless substance of Reality.
He only knows who conquers evil; he,
Who masters self, passes beyond the dim
Uncertain light of faith, and on him breaks
The light of Perfect Knowledge which enfolds
Emancipation, gladness, perfect peace.

Eolaus. I know that sorrow follows passion; know
That grief and emptiness and heartaches wait
Upon all earthly joys; so am I sad;
Yet Truth must be, and, being, can be found;
And though I am in sorrow, this I know—
I shall be glad when I have found the Truth.

Prophet. There is no gladness like the joy of Truth.
The pure in heart swim in a sea of bliss
That evermore nor sorrow knows, nor pain;
For who can see the Cosmos and be sad?
To know is to be happy; they rejoice
Who have attained Perfection; these are they
Who live, and know, and realize the Truth.

Eolaus. I strive for that Perfection; shall I reach
The Heights of Blessed Vision?

Prophet. Comfort ye,
The Heights of Blessed Vision ye shall reach.

Eolaus. Yet how, and when, and where? I am confused.
The Way is near, and yet I see it not!

Prophet. He must be friendly with the worm and toad
Who would be the companion of the wise,
And know the Cosmic Splendour; he must stoop
Who seeks to stand; must fall who fain would rise;
Must know the low, ascending to the high:
He who would know the Great, must not disdain
To diligently wait upon the small:
He wisdom finds who finds humility.

Eolaus. Speak on, O Prophet! I attend thy words,

Prophet. The beasts can neither bend nor stand erect
Being beasts,—abandon bestial tendencies;
But man can bend, and man can stand erect,
Being man,— embrace pure thoughts and stainless deeds;
Here is deliverance. Man's redemption lies
In man himself, yet is not born of self,
But takes its rise in Truth: man can achieve
He findeth Truth who findeth self-control.

Eolaus. When I have found the meaning of thy
words, I know I shall be wise as thou art wise;
But now I hear thee, and yet hear thee not.

Prophet. Thou wilt perceive the substance of my words,
And understand their meaning, when they stir
That meaning in thyself, and in thy mind
Stand clear and well-reflected; thou canst know
Only by subjugation of thyself,

And practice of the highest: all that's real
Is inward; outward things are fleeting shows,
Vain and illusory, holding nor rest
Nor refuge for the wise: obey the Right,
And wrong shall ne'er again assail thy peace,
Nor error hurt thee more: attune thy heart
To Purity, and thou shalt reach the Place
Where sorrow is not, and all evil ends.
The Holy Ones know not the name of sin;
Goodness and Truth make glad the good and true:
The Perfect Ones behold the Perfect Law;
Struggle and strife are ended in the Truth.
All things are holy to the holy mind,
All uses are legitimate and pure,
All occupations blest arid sanctified,
And every day a Sabbath.

Eolaus. I perceive
Some glimmering of a Light transcending light,
Some outline of a mighty Principle
More beautiful than beauty; see some dim
Appearing of the vision of a Life
Vaster than life: the Cosmos is sublime !
My eyes will open, I shall see the Truth,
And, seeing, shall be glad for evermore !

Prophet. Be mindful, or the thought that soars will sink:
Be lowly, patient, well-instructed; hold
Thyself in check-, by many single steps
All journeys reach completion: as the tree
That rears its stately head toward the sky—
Bestowing shade and shelter—issued from
A tiny seed, and, waiting patiently
Upon the law of growth, it came to be
The thing majestic that it now appears,—
So wisdom from a single act of good
Well-planted, watched, and watered, comes at last
To its sublime proportions.

Eolaus. I will tend
The plant of wisdom with all diligence,
And watch its growth toward perfection.
Show me the unobserved and lowly Way;

Let praise, reward, and popularity
Be no more sweet to me, and no more sought;
Let self be blotted out, I seek the Truth.

Prophet. Now listen, and attend:—the pigeons pick
Holes in the buildings, and the storm o'erturns
That they had weakened: little failings eat
Holes in the citadel of Character
Which, weakened thus, cannot withstand the storms
Of circumstance, but weakly falls before
Tempestuous temptations. As the bee
Buildeth the honeycomb, the bird its nest,
The builder his strong house, e'en bit by bit,
Straw unto straw, and stone laid upon stone,
Until the finished thing and perfect whole
Crowns effort with success,—so the wise man.
By adding thought to thought and deed to deed
In ways of good, buildeth his character.
Little by little he accomplishes
His noble ends; in quiet patience works
Diligently, while others sleep, or slake
Their hot desires in riot; nowise moved
From his main purpose by perplexities,
Falls, errors, failures, difficulties, pains,
Daily he builds into his heart and mind
Pure thoughts, high aspirations, selfless deeds,
Until at last the edifice of Truth
Is finished, and behold! there rises and appears
The Temple of Perfection.

Eolaus. I have found
The little Gate mean and moss-grown which leads
Into a dark, despised, neglected Way
Which, further, leads to glorious esplanades
And heights of Splendour; foolish men avoid
The lowly, and thereby the lofty lose;
Despise the small, and the majestical
Miss, and see not. Prophet of Good and Truth,
Wisely and well hast thou instructed me;
Thou hast revealed to me the Path of Peace;
My eyes are opened, and at last I see
Thy lowly Way, and I will enter in.

Prophet. The Perfect Way awaits thy strenuous tread;
Behold where rise, precipitous, yet grand,
The Hills of Virtue; higher, and beyond,
The Peaks of Blessedness; and yet again,
Upon the lofty Summits of the Truth,
Where clouds and darkness are not, and where rests
Eternal Splendour; there, abiding Joy
Awaits thy coming. Onward, and disperse
The dark delusions of thy self! Evil
Is Good denied, is darkness and no more.
Let self be nothing, and the Truth be all;
Thus conquer pain: acquire serenity;
Wisdom accompanies tranquillity;
The self-subdued the fadeless Glory know:
Be watchful, fearless, faithful, patient, pure:
By earnest meditation sound the depths
Profound of life, and scale the heights sublime
Of Love and Wisdom. He who does not find
The Way of Meditation, cannot reach
Emancipation and enlightenment.
But thou wilt find the Way of Holy Thought;
With mind made calm and steadfast, thou wilt see
The Permanent amid the mutable,
The Truth eternal in the things that change:
Thou wilt behold the Perfect Law: Cosmos
From Chaos rises when the conquered self
Lies underneath man's heel: Love be thy strength;
Look on the passion-tortured multitudes,
And have compassion on them; know their pain
By thy long sorrow ended. Thou wilt come
To perfect peace, and so wilt bless the world,
Leading unto the High and Holy Way
The feet of them that seek.—And now I go
To my Abode; go thou unto thy work.

Eolaus. Prophet of Peace, I go: and unto Thee,
Spirit of Truth, I come. To all the world,
And all that lives, for evermore be peace.

Cosmos

I am; Perfection is, and Peace;
 Evil is gone, beholding Me;

And they from sin and sorrow cease
 Who look upon my Symmetry.
When fault and failure find my Form,
 Lo, fault and failure are no more !
I am the sunshine and the storm,
 The whisper, and the ocean's roar !
The creeping action that deceives,
 The lie, the theft, the murderer's ire,
All these my Crucible receive,
 They burn in my Celestial Fire.
All superstitions, errors, wiles,
 The crawling craft, the cruel lust,
All that debases and defiles
 I grind, and scatter in in the dust.
The Nations rise, the Empires fall,
 And I eternally rehearse,
To scene and strain majestical,
 The Drama of the Universe.
The Eons pass, the systems pale,
 Unchanged their changes behold;
They listen, and I tell my Tale;
 I all their fleeting forms enfold.
Who knoweth Me, becometh Me;
 Who hath my Vision finds release
From Darkness and Captivity.
 I am; Perfection is, and Peace.

Miscellaneous poems

Buddha

Under Mount Ratnagira's western shade,
Weary and worn with his long search for Truth,
Sorrowing, unsatisfied, disconsolate,
Sat Buddha, knowing not where he should turn
To find the Truth that he had so long sought—
The Truth that maketh steadfast, strong, and pure,
The Truth that bringeth peace and blessed rest.
The Schools had failed him, the philosophies,
Hoary and ancient, had not stilled the cry
Of passion in his heart; and passion's child,
Sorrow, was with him still; the scriptures, creeds,

Proud pillars of the State, had failed to bear
The weight of his great woe, crumbling away
Under temptation, leaving him the prey
Still of desire and pain and clouded mind.
Mortifications he had tried, and they
Had left him strengthless, wan, wanting the Truth;
And now he seemed as one defeated, borne
Upon the stream of Fate, helpless, alone.

But while the Buddha brooded in the shade,
Suddenly on his ear there fell a cry,
A sob of pain, a pitiful strange sigh;
Whereat he rose, and left the shade, and sought
(He scarce knew why, but that there leaped within
His sorrowing heart a mighty unknown love)
Whence came the cry; and presently he saw,
Upon the road, 'mid thirsty clouds of dust,
Under the fierce blaze of the Indian sun,
A shepherd, driving hard a flock of sheep;
And in the rear there lagged a little lamb
With wounded feet, bleating most piteously,
The while the ewe, with anguish deep and sore,
Cried o'er her little one, knowing that she
Was helpless to relieve her.

When Buddha saw
The piteous spectacle, compassion slew
His own deep sorrow; and he straightway took
The wounded lamb, and bore it in his arms,
Saying, 'Vain are the strivings of the soul
After vain knowledge; vain the learned lore
That hath not pity in it; vain is life
That hath not love; and whatsoe'er is false,
And what uncertain, though it seemeth true,
This thing is true, that I should pity thee.
The priests who pray and read, and read and pray,
Die in their sins at last, and do not find
The Love I mourn for, the deep Truth I seek;
And better where it that I ease thy pain
Than pray with them, and seek and never find.
Thee will I love; yea, I will pity thee
Whom none will pity; thee will I relieve;
Tired of the soulless theories of men,

I, Buddha, will stoop to thee, thou dumb, weak thing,
Whom men despise, knowing that this is true,
Whate'er is doubtful, and whate'er unsure,
Pity and Love are right; what ever fades
And perishes, Compassion will not fade,
And Love will never perish." So he took
Into his arms the weary, wounded thing
Which nestled in his bosom, and became
Quiet and peaceful; and the anxious ewe
Walked by his side, looking into his face,
Glad that her lamb had found those blessed arms:
And so she walked, and dumbly worshipped him,
Knowing him Buddha, the compassionate.

And Buddha in that hour entered the Way
Which he had vainly sought in schools and creeds;
Entered the Path which no philosophy
Leads unto, and which none shall ever find
But by sweet deeds of Love, forgetting self;
And in his heart there grew a holy Love;
And in his mind a knowledge new and strange;
And his whole being felt a painless peace;
Sorrow and pain were not; and then he knew
hat he had found the holy Truth at last.

And from thenceforward Buddha lived the Truth,
And taught its practice; and from far and near
Came men and women who had sought the Truth,
And at his feet they sat and worshipped him,
Learning of love and pity; finding bliss
And peace that cannot fail; and him they called
Deliverer, Redeemer, Blessed Lord.
And even they who understood not, sensed
Faintly this truth which one day they should know:—
Better than learning is a loving heart;
And to give comfort to one wounded lamb
Is higher than the wisdom of the schools,
And greater than the world's philosophy.

If men only understood

If men only understood
That the wrong act of a Brother
Should not call from them another,

But should be annulled with kindness,
That *their* eyes should aid his blindness,
They would find the Heavenly Portal
Leading on to Love immortal—
 If they only understood.

If men only understood
That *their* wrong can never smother
The wrong-doing of another;
That by hatred hate increases,
And by Good all evil ceases,
They would cleanse their hearts and actions.
Banish thence all vile detractions—
 If they only understood.

If men only understood
That the heart that sins *must* sorrow,
That the hateful mind to-morrow
Reaps its barren harvest, weeping,
Starving, resting not, nor sleeping;
Tenderness would fill their being.
They would see with Pity's seeing—
 If they only understood.

If men only understood
All the emptiness and aching
Of the sleeping mid the waking
Of the souls they judge so blindly,
Of the hearts they pierce unkindly.
They, with gentler words and feeling,
Would apply the balm of healing—
 If they only understood.

If men only understood
That their hatred and resentment
Slays their peace and sweet contentment
Hurts themselves, helps not another,
Does not cheer one lonely Brother,
They would seek the better doing
Of good deeds which leaves no rueing-—
 If they only understood.

If men only understood
How Love conquers; how prevailing

Is its might, grim hate assailing;
How Compassion endeth sorrow,
Maketh wise, and doth not borrow
Pain of passion; they would ever
Live in Love, in hatred never—
 If they only understood.

Practice and perception

Questioning Life and Destiny and Truth,
I sought the dark and labyrinthine Sphinx,
Who spake to me this strange and wondrous thing:—
" Concealment only lies in blinded eyes,
And God alone can see the Form of God."

I sought to solve this hidden mystery
Vainly by paths of blindness and of pain,
But when I found the Way of Love and Peace,
Concealment ceased, and I was blind no more:
Then saw I God e'en with the eyes of God.

Liberty

The unwise say, " Our sufferings are unjust,
Our pains and woes rise from the scattered dust
Of sinful ancestors; we are not free;
Our fathers robbed us of our liberty
By what they did; and we are weak and frail
Because they erred; they fell, and we must fail.

" Our drunkenness comes from their love of wine;
Our lusts their revels made; and we divine
Our manifold diseases by the ways
In which they walked; and as they trod the maze
Made by their feet, so we must likewise tread,
For we are bound and driven by the dead."

Thy sins are thine, O man ! and from thy deeds
Thy life, with all its weal and woe, proceeds;
By self, and not by others, thou art bound;
In thine own will and heart the root is found
Of all thy lack of peace; open thou thine eyes,
Leave the dead past, and look within; be wise.

Make pure thy heart, and thou wilt make thy life
Rich, sweet, and beautiful, unmarred by strife;

Guard well thy mind, and, noble, strong, and free,
Nothing shall harm, disturb or conquer thee;
For all thy foes are in thy heart and mind;
There also thy salvation thou wilt find.

Mind is the Master-power that moulds and makes.
And Man is Mind and evermore he takes
The Tool of Thought, and, shaping what he wills,
Brings forth a thousand joys, a thousand ills:—
He thinks in secret, and it comes to pass;
Environment is but his looking-glass.

In his own heart he fosters dark desires,
Or strives for good, or loftily aspires;
In his own life he reaps what he has sown,
Or pain or peace, he garners in his own.
Thou man, that bowest to heredity,
Know this—the Law of life is Liberty,

By Thought we rise; by Thought we fall; by Thought
We stand or go: all destiny is wrought
By its swift potency; and he who stands
Master of Thought, and his desires commands,
Willing and weaving thoughts of Love and Might,
Shapes his high end in Truth's unerring Light.

Long I sought thee

Long I sought thee, Spirit holy,
 Master Spirit, meek and lowly;
Sought thee with a silent sorrow, brooding o'er the woes of
men;
 Vainly sought thy yoke of meekness
 'Neath the weight of woe and weakness;
Finding not, yet in my failing, seeking o'er and o'er again.

In unrest and doubt and sadness
 Dwelt I, yet I knew thy Gladness
Waited somewhere; somewhere greeted torn and sorrowing
hearts like mine;
 Knew that somehow I should find thee,
 Leaving sin and woe behind me,
And at last thy Love would bid me enter into Rest divine.

Hatred, mockery, and reviling
 Scorched my seeking soul, defiling
That which should have been thy Temple, wherein thou
should'st move and dwell;
 Praying, striving, hoping, calling;
 Suffering, sorrowing in my falling,
Still I sought thee, groping blindly in the gloomy depths of hell.

And I sought thee till I found thee;
 And the dark Powers all around me
Fled and left me silent, peaceful, brooding o'er thy holy
themes;
 From within me and without me
 Fled they when I ceased to doubt thee;
And I found thee in thy Glory, mighty Master of my dreams !

Yea, I found thee, Spirit holy,
 Beautiful and pure and lowly;
Found thy Joy and Peace and Gladness; found thee in thy
House of Rest;
 Found thy strength in Love and Meekness,
 And my pain and woe and weakness
Left me, and I walked the Pathway trodden only by the blest.

Reality

I see men gaze upon the distant skies
 Of ideals inaccessible and vain;
And miss the Holy Way which near them lies—
 The hourly conquest over sin and pain.

I see uplifted and imploring hands
 Aching with emptiness; I see the cause,
Self-made, of man's long sorrow; see his bands
 Self-wrought, self-bound; I see the broken laws.

Wisdom lies hidden in our common life,
 And he will find it who shall rightly ask;
Where springs the fretful fever and the strife
 There Truth abides—e'en in the daily task.

Behold where Love Eternal rests concealed !
 (The deathless Love that seemed so far away!)
E'en in the lowly heart; it stands revealed
 To him who lives the sinless life to-day.

Wrapped in our nearest duty is the Key
 Which shall unlock for us the Heavenly Gate;
Unveiled, the Heavenly Vision he shall sec,
 Who cometh not too early nor too late.

The glory of the Truth no Future veils
 From tear - stained eyes; no Past obliterates,
For toil - worn feet, the narrow, weed - grown trails
 Which wind through common ways to joyful Gates.

Where'er we go immortal splendour goes;
 But eyes, self-blinded, look and cannot see;
Th' Eternal Glory shines upon man's woes,
 Piercing the dark night of his misery.

Lo ! where the shadowless Effulgence gleams—
 In tasks well done, in stainless thoughts and deeds,
In words of love and pity, not in dreams
 Of sky - bound glories holding future needs.

Peace cometh only to the peaceful soul;
 Love, painless, nestles in the Love-born heart;
Joy springs where self is sunken for the whole;
 From conquered sins immortal beauties start.

Our task is with us, and the Path Sublime,
 Rising from swamps of self, through Duty's way,
Cuts its clear course up the steep hills of Time
 Unto the splendour of the Perfect Day.

To-morrow and to-day

In the dark land of To-morrow
 I dwelt with pain and sorrow,
And I sighed for joys and blessings that escaped me as I ran;
 And the darkness gathered round me,
 For the morrow ever found me
Living in "What I ought to do," and not in *what I can.*

And I sought for loving-kindness
 In the dim, dark haunts of blindness;
In the lightless caves of self I searched for blessedness and
rest;
 And I reached out hands appealing,
 Sadly groped for light and healing,
Striving for " what I want to have, " not *what is true and best.*

Then I found that selfish hoping,
 Darkly seeking, blindly groping
In vain wishing and regretting chased life's glory from my brow;
 So I ceased from selfish fretting,
 Turned to Love, and, self-forgetting,
Left " what I hope to get and keep," for *what I will be now.*

So I fled from self and sorrow,
 Left the dark land of To-morrow,
And thought of what kind deeds to do, what loving words to say;
 And the light of peace and gladness
 Chased away the clouds of sadness,
For I lost the past and future in the bright world of To-day.

Star of wisdom

Star that of the birth of Vishnu,
Birth of Krishna, Buddha, Jesus,
Told the wise ones, Heavenward looking,
Waiting, watching for thy gleaming.
In the darkness of the night-time.
In the starless gloom of midnight;
Shining Herald of the coming
Of the kingdom of the righteous:
Teller of the mystic story
Of the lowly birth of Godhead
In the stable of the passions,
In the manger of the mind-soul;
Silent singer of the secret
Of compassion deep and holy
To the heart with sorrow burdened,
To the soul with waiting weary:—
Star of all-surpassing brightness,
Thou again dost deck the midnight;
Thou again dost cheer the wise ones
Watching in the creedal darkness,
Weary of the endless battle
With the grinding blades of error;
Tired of lifeless, useless idols,
Of the dead forms of religions;
Spent with watching for thy shining;

Thou hast ended their despairing;
Thou hast lighted up their pathway;
Thou hast brought again the old Truths
To the hearts of all thy Watchers;
To the souls of them that love thee
Thou dust speak of Joy and Gladness,
Of the Peace that endeth sorrow.
Blessed are they that can see thee,
Weary wanderers in the Night-time;
Blessed they who feel the throbbing,
In their bosoms feel the pulsing
Of a deep Love stirred within them
By the great power of thy shining.
Let us learn thy lesson truly;
Learn it faithfully and humbly;
Learn it meekly, wisely, gladly,
Ancient star of holy Vishnu,
Light of Krishna, Buddha, Jesus.

Would you scale the highest heaven

Would you scale the highest heaven,
 Would you pierce the lowest hell,—
Live in dreams of constant beauty,
 Or in basest thinkings dwell.

For your thoughts are heaven above you,
 And your thoughts are hell below;
Bliss is not, except in thinking,
 Torment naught but thought can know.

Worlds would vanish but for thinking;
 Glory is not but in dreams;
And the Drama of the ages
 From the Thought Eternal streams.

Dignity and shame and sorrow,
 Pain and anguish, love and hate
Are but maskings of the mighty
 Pulsing Thought that governs Fate.

As the colours of the rainbow
 Make the one uncoloured beam,
So the universal changes
 Make the One Eternal Dream.

And the Dream is all within you,
 And the Dreamer waileth long
For the Morning to awake him
 To the living thought and strong.

That shall make the ideal real,
 Make to vanish dreams of hell
In the highest, holiest heaven
 Where the pure and perfect dwell.

Evil is the thought that thinks it;
 Good, the thought that makes it so;
Light and darkness, sin and pureness
 Likewise out of thinking grow.

Dwell in thought upon the Grandest,
 And the Grandest you shall see;
Fix your mind upon the Highest,
 And the Highest you shall be.

To them that seek the highest good

To them that seek the highest Good
 All things subserve the wisest ends;
 Naught comes as ill, and wisdom lends
Wings to all shapes of evil brood.

The darkening sorrow veils a Star
 That waits to shine with gladsome light;
 Hell waits on heaven; and after night
Comes golden glory from afar.

Defeats are steps by which we climb
 With purer aim to nobler ends;
 Loss leads to gain, and joy attends
True footsteps up the hills of time.

Pain lead to paths of holy bliss,
 To thoughts and words and deeds divine;
 And clouds that gloom and rays that shine,
Along life's upward highway kiss.

Misfortune does but cloud the way
 Whose end and summit in the sky
 Of bright success, sunkiss'd and high,
Awaits our seeking and our stay.

The heavy pall of doubts and fears
 That clouds the Valley of our hopes,
 The shades with which the spirit copes,
 The bitter harvesting of tears,

The heartaches, miseries, and griefs,
 The bruisings born of broken ties,
 All these are steps by which we rise
To living ways of sound beliefs.

Love, pitying, watchful, runs to meet
 The Pilgrim from the Land of Fate;
 All glory and all good await
The coming of obedient feet.

One thing lacking

E'en at the Master's holy feet, low kneeling,
 Came one who knew nor wordly want nor stress
Yet sad with fruitless search for Truth, and feeling
 Perchance the Teacher of the world might bless
Then asked he softly, and with humble pleading,—
 "Good Master, canst Thou calm my inward strife?
Show me the lofty highway of Thy leading;
 What shall I do to gain Eternal Life?"

Then He, the Lord of Life, looked down in kindness
 Upon the Kneeling form, and, answering, said,—
"Thou knowest the commandments, be not mindless
 Of these, and thou shalt live, though thou wert dead."
Replied the Kneeling one,—"All these things keeping
 From my youth up, I sought Thee out this day,
Yet still I wander unawakened, sleeping;
 I have not found the high and holy Way."

Yet lackest thou one thing, yield thy desiring,"
 (Thus spake the Master), "do not grasp, but give;
Sell that thou holdest, and, with free aspiring,
 Come, follow Me, and thou shalt truly live;
For whoso follows Me, all selfish clinging
 Yielding with pure and undivided mind
Shall nothing lack; yea, for his earthly bringing
 Surely the Heavenly Treasure he shall find."
Now he who knelt was very rich, and cherished
 His earthly treasure in his inmost heart;
And even there his spirit paused and perished,
 Losing renunciation's better part:

Noble but not complete, the Master leaving
 To cleave unto his perishable day,
He chose the path of passing things and grieving,
 And, sorrow-stricken, went his lonely way.

Yashas

 Lo, in the night, when all the world was sleeping,
 Yashas, the noble and aspiring youth,
Pondering upon the world's great sorrow, weeping,
 Searched for the holy pathway unto Truth.
" I search in vain," said he, " and will betake me
 Unto the Blessed One, and seek release;
Healer of sorrow, he perchance will make me
 Partaker in his deep, Nirvanic peace."

 Then came the youth, with footsteps fast and faster,
 Unto the Blessed Teacher of mankind,
And, weeping, fell before the Holy Master,
 Saying, "Great Lord, I seek and cannot find.
How great is my distress and tribulation !
 Thou knowest all my sorrow and my pain;
Give me the holy balm of thy salvation,
 Let me depart not from thy side again."

The Blessed One, seeing his perturbation,
 Spake softly thus unto the gentle youth
" Lo, here is no distress, no tabulation;
 Come unto Me, and I will show you Truth
The Truth will bring you joy, dispelling sadness,
 And as the night before the light of day
Flees and departs, e'en so your rising gladness
 Sorrow and pain and care will chase away."

Then spake He of things pure and high and holy
 Giving full freely of His wisdom's store,
And Yashas, listening, rapt, all meek and 'lowly
 Drank deeply of the Master's wondrous lore;
And lo! the cooling breath of Wisdom o'er him
 Stole softly, fanning all his care to rest;
Sorrow departed, and Compassion bore him
 Unto the Path the Master's feet had prest.

The lowly way

All ways are waiting for my feet to tread,
The light and dark, the living and the dead,

The broad and narrow way, the high and low,
The good and bad, and with quick step or slow,
I now may enter any way I will,
And find, by walking, which is good, which ill.

And all good things my wand'ring feet await,
If I but come, with vow inviolate,
Unto the narrow, high and holy way
Of heart-born purity, and therein stay;
Walking, secure from him who taunts and scorns,
To flowery meads, across the path of thorns.

And I may stand where health, success, and power
Await my coming, if, each fleeting hour,
I cling to love and patience: and abide
With stainlessness; and never step aside
From high integrity; so shall I see
At last the land of immortality.

And I may seek and find; I may achieve;
I may not claim, but, losing, may retrieve,
The Law bends not for me, but I must bend
Unto the Law, if I would reach the end
Of my afflictions, if I would restore
My soul to Light and Life and weep no more.

Not mine the arrogant and selfish claim
To all good things; be mine the lowly aim
To seek and find, to know and comprehend,
And wisdom-ward all holy footsteps wend
Nothing is mine to claim or to command,
But all is mine to know and understand.

The music of the sea

I love to hear the music of the sea,
 As, playing on the everlasting shore,
Its strange, profound, and mystic melody,
 It chants the soul of man for evermore.

It sings of wreckful passion when it beats
 With unrestrained wildness on the rocks;
Then with succeeding sorrow it retreats,
 Sobbing o'er pain of self- inflicted shocks.

Of martyrdom and silent pain it speaks
 When, dumbly moaning, languidly it rolls;

And weirdly wails, as on the rocks it breaks,
  The deadness and despair of human souls.

Its scintillations on the pebbly beach,
  Mingling with sunshine and the playful breeze,
Are bubbling merriment and mirth that reach
  No deeper than the sensuous vision sees.

When, scarcely murmuring, placidly it lies,
  It whispers of the silent heart of peace;
Of that unutterable state where dies
  Passion, and all our human sorrows cease.

Playful, perturbed, peaceful, tempestuous,
  Reflected in thy heart, thy peace, thy strife,
Is the strange passion and peace in us,
  The madness and the wisdom of our life.

Thou symbol of the human soul, O sea!
  I love to hear thee, on the lonely shore
Chanting thy everlasting melody,
  Singing the soul of man for evermore.

Love's conquest

I stood upon the shore, and saw the rocks
  Resist the onslaught of the mighty sea,
And when I thought how all the countless shocks
  They had withstood through an eternity,
I said, " To wear away this solid main
The ceaseless efforts of the waves are vain."

But when I thought how they the rocks had rent,
  And saw the sand and shingles at my feet
(Poor passive remnants of resistance spent)
  Tumbled and tossed where they the waters meet,
Then saw I ancient landmarks' neath the waves,
And knew the waters held the stones their slaves.

I saw the mighty work the waters wrought
  By patient softness and unceasing flow;
How they the proudest promontory brought
  Unto their feet, and massy hills laid low;
How the soft drops the adamantine wall
Conquered at last, and brought it to its fall.

And then I knew that hard, resisting sin
  Should yield at last to Love's soft ceaseless roll

Coming and going, ever flowing in
 Upon the proud rocks of the human soul;
That all resistance should be spent and past,
And every heart yield unto it at last.

To my daughter Nora on her tenth birthday

Since when thou earnest, with thy native charms,
A weeping infant to thy mother's arms,
Ten fleeting years have lifted up thy head
Unto my breast; ten years of love are fled,
But all their store of innocence and bliss
Remains with thee; thy mother's and my kiss
Seal it for ever thine! Those guileless ways
Which, walking, have filled up thy tender days,
May'st thou for ever keep; may thy pure heart
Keep always pure, that no unholy dart
Pierce it with anguish; may remorse and pain
Shrink from thy hallowed presence, and no stain
Soil thy white robes of peace. O ! be thou sure
Bliss follows in the footsteps of the pure.
And whatsoe'er shall tempt of wrong or strife,
Hold fast the rare gem of a blameless life;
Nor lose, nor lightly hold, but bind to thee
The priceless jewel of thy purity.

The inward purity

Find ye that life is anguish, and that self-love is a chain
That binds thy quivering soul, and cuts with biting stings of
pain?
Grieve ye where Slander's serpents trail beneath fair flowers
of Trust?
Or weep where Friendship buried lies 'neath Hatred's fulsome
dust?
Then listen,—Selfish sweets are brief, and fleeting self-hood's
ties,
But there abides a fadeless Love, a Life that never dies;
A path there is which Serpent slime hath never yet defiled,
Where weary feet find rest and peace, and are no more
beguiled:
And that pure Love and Life are his whose inmost heart is free.
From unforgiveness, judgment false, and self and enmity;

And that fair Path of Peace he walks whose memory holds no stain
Of injuries past; that blameless heart hath reached the end of pain.

Self-sacrifice

Great glory crowns the heights of hope by arduous struggle won;
Bright honour rounds the hoary head that mighty works hath done;
Fair riches come to him who strives in ways of golden gain,
And fame enshrines his name who works with genius-glowing brain:
But greater glory waits for him who, in the bloodless strife
'Gainst self and wrong, adopts, in love, the sacrificial life;
And brighter honour rounds the brow of him who, 'mid the scorns
Of blind idolaters of self, accepts the crown of thorns;
And fairer, purer riches come to him greatly strives
To walk in ways of love and truth to sweeten human lives;
And he who serveth well mankind exchanges fleeting fame
For Light eternal, Joy and Peace, and robes of heavenly flame.

I take refuge in truth

I come to thee, O Master! on thy breast
 I lay my weary head; I lave thy feet
With tears and kisses, travail of my quest;
 I bring my aching heart and sore defeat,
And seek thy holy joy and perfect rest.

Place thou thy hand upon my burning brow;
 Soothe thou my soul, and bid my sins depart;
I ask thy sweet salvation even now;
 Thy rest I seek to ease my throbbing heart;
Thou art the Truth, to thee I cling and bow.

Thou changest not amid Earth's changing scenes;
 All worldly joys, strong passions that decay,
The sordid thought, the action that demeans,
 These are not thee, and they will pass away:
On thy abiding strength my spirit leans.

Lead thou my feet unto thy Holy Place;
 I take thy chastening; thy great love I sec;

Thy rod I kiss, and in my deep disgrace,
 With longing, humble heart I cling to thee,
Knowing thou wilt not turn away thy face.

I, truth, am thy redeemer

I, Truth, am thy Redeemer, come to Me;
 Lay down thy sin and pain wild unrest;
And I will calm thy spirit's stormy sea,
 Pouring the oil of peace upon thy breast:
Friendless and lone—lo, I abide with thee.

Defeated and deserted, cast away;
 What refuge hast thou? Whither canst thou fly?
Upon My changeless breast thy burdens lay;
 I am thy certain refuge, even I:
All things are passing; I alone can stay.

Lo I, the Great Forsaken, am the Friend
 Of the forsaken; I, whom men despise,
The weak, the helpless, and despised defend;
 I gladden aching hearts and weeping eyes:
Rest thou in Me, I am thy sorrow's end.

Lovers and friends and wealth, pleasures and fame—
 These fail and change, and pass into decay;
But my Love does not change; and in thy blame
 I blame thee not, nor turn My face away:
In My calm bosom hide thy sin and shame.

The white robe

The White Robe of the Heart Invisible
 Is stained with sin and sorrow, grief and pain,
And all repentant pools and springs of prayer
 Shall not avail to wash it white again.

While in the path of ignorance I walk,
 The stains of error will not cease to cling;
Defilements mark the crooked path of self,
 Where anguish lurks and disappointments sting.

Knowledge and wisdom only can avail
 To purify and make my garment clean,
For therein lie love's waters; therein rests
 Peace undisturbed, eternal, and serene.

Sin and repentance is the path of pain,
 Knowledge and wisdom is the path of Peace;
By the near way of practice I will find
 Where bliss begins, how pains and sorrows cease.

Self shall depart, and Truth shall take its place;
 The Changeless One, the Indivisible
Shall take up His abode in me, and cleanse
 The white Robe of the Heart Invisible.

The righteous man

No harmful shaft can reach the righteous man,
 Standing erect amid the storms of hate,
Defying hurt and injury and ban,
 Surrounded by the trembling slaves of Fate.

Majestic in the strength of silent power,
 Serene he stands, nor changes not nor turns;
Patient and firm in suffering's darkest hour,
 Time bends to him, and death and doom he spurns.

Wrath's lurid lightnings round about him play,
 And hell's deep thunders roll about his head;
Yet heeds he not, for him they cannot slay
 Who stands whence earth and time and space are fled.

Sheltered by deathless love, what fear hath he?
 Armoured in changeless Truth, what can he know
Of loss and gain? Knowing eternity,
 He moves not whilst the shadows come and go.

Call him immortal, call him Truth and Light
 And splendour of prophetic majesty
Who bideth thus amid the powers of Night,
 Clothed with the glory of divinity.

Choice

The will to evil and the will to Good
 Are both within thee: which wilt thou employ?
Thou knowest what is right and what is wrong;
 Which wilt thou love and foster? which destroy?

Thou art the chooser of thy thoughts and deeds;
 Thou art the maker of thine inward state;

The power is thine to be what thou wilt be;
  Thou buildest Truth and Love, or lies and hate.

If thou dost choose the evil, loving self,
  Thy cries and prayers for Good shall all be vain;
Thy thought and act bringeth thee good or ill;
  Deep in thy heart thou makest joy and pain.

As thou pursuest Good, striving to make
  Evil depart, thou shalt rejoice and say,—
" Lo! Light and Love and Peace attend on me;
  Truth fadeth not, and Good abounds away."

Choose as thou wilt thy thoughts and words and deeds,
  And as thou choosest so shall be thy life;
The will to Good shall bring thee Joy and Peace,
  The will to evil, wretchedness and strife.

Truth triumphant

There is no height to which thou canst not climb;
  There is no grandeur that thou may'st not view,
If thou wilt reach beyond the things of Time,
  Unto the Pure, the Beautiful, the True.

There is no saintly vision, no glad sight
  Of seer, nor no dream of holy sage
But may be thine; nay, is thy heavenly right,
  If thou wilt claim thy regal appanage.

There is no sin but thou may'st overthrow;
  There is no vileness that, octopus-like,
Binds thee its victim, but thou soon canst know
  The way and weapon thy strong foe to strike.

Thou art not framed for sin and grief and shame;
  Thou art not bent to grovel in the mire;
But thou art made erect, and given a name,
  Hast hands to reach, and spirit to aspire.

Glory and strength and triumph — these are thine;
  Rise up, and conquer every inward foe;
Behold the heavens, how radiantly they shine !
  Stand up and strike, O conqueror of woe!

O thou who would'st teach!

O thou who would'st teach men of Truth!
  Hast thou passed through the desert of doubt?

Art thou purged by the fires of sorrow? hath ruth
 The fiends of opinion cast out
Of thy human heart? Is thy soul so fair
That no false thought can ever harbour there?

O thou who would'st teach men of Love !
 Hast thou passed through the place of despair?
Hast thou wept through the dark night of grief? does it move
 (Now freed from its sorrow and care)
Thy human heart to pitying gentleness,
Looking on wrong, and hate, and ceaseless stress?

O thou who would'st teach men of Peace!
 Hast thou crossed the wide ocean of strife?
Hast thou found on the Shores of the Silence, release
 From all the wild unrest of life?
From thy human heart hath all striving gone,
Leaving but Truth, and Love, and Peace alone?

If thou would'st right the world

If thou would'st right the world,
And banish all its evils and its woes,
 Make its wild places bloom,
And its drear deserts blossom as the rose,—
 Then right thyself.

If thou would'st turn the world
From its long, lone captivity in sin,
 Restore all broken hearts,
Slay grief, and let sweet consolation in, —
 Turn thou thyself.

It thou would'st cure the world
Of its long sickness, end its grief and pain,
 Bring in all-healing Joy,
And give to the afflicted rest again,—
 Then cure thyself.

If thou would'st wake the world
Out of its dream of death and dark'ning strifc,
 Bring it to Love and Peace,
And Light and brightness of immortal Life,—
 Wake thou thyself.

What of the night?

What of the night, O Watchman ! see'st thou yet
 The glimmering dawn upon the mountain heights
 The golden Herald of the Light of lights,
Are his fair feet upon the hilltops set?

Cometh he yet to chase away the gloom,
 And with it all the demons of the Night?
 Strike yet his darting rays upon thy sight?
Hear'st thou his voice, the sound of error's doom?

The Morning cometh, lover of the Light;
 E'en now He gilds with gold the mountain's brow,
 Dimly I see the path whereon e'en now
His shining feet are set toward the Night.

Darkness shall pass away, and all the things
 That love the darkness, and that hate the Light
 Shall disappear for ever with the Night:
Rejoice! for thus the speeding Herald sings.

Knowledge

We find the Good by being good, the True
 By being true, the Real by dissolving
Our fond illusions, thereby piercing through
 Shadow, and knowing substance. By resolving,
We can attain, and by attaining, know;
 And, knowing, who shall cause us grief or harm?
What trembling victim of the world's vain show
 Shall pierce the armoured heart, or foil the arm
Of him whose Shield is Wisdom? What event,
 What circumstance, what mutability
Can shake the Changeless? And whoso hath lent
 His life with Changeless Good, stands steadfastly
In Knowledge, fearing nothing, hating naught;
His heart and mind Love-fashioned, Wisdom-wrought.

The end of evil

All evil passes from us when we find
The Way of Good; when word and deed and mind
Are shaped to Truth and Wisdom; then we see
The end of bondage and captivity.

All good is ever with us; we but want
Wisdom to take it; we are poor and scant
Only in lacking wisdom; that acquired,
The good is ours that we so long desired.

Be stilt any soul and know that peace is thine;
Be steadfast, heart, and know that strength divine
Belongs to thee: cease from thy turmoil, mind,
And thou the Everlasting Rest shalt find.

Man divine

Man is superior to sin and shame,
 Evil and error he will yet dethrone,
The beasts within he will o'ercome and tame,
 The brute will pass, the Angel will be known;
Yea, even now the Man divine appears,
Crowned with conquest, victor o'er all fears.

Hail to thee, Man divine ! the conqueror
 Of sin and shame and sorrow; no more weak,
Wormlike and grovelling art thou; no, nor
 Wilt thou again bow down to things that wreak
Scourgings and death upon thee; thou dost rise
Triumphant in thy strength; good, pure, and wise.

Patience

Why this fierce struggle to achieve thine ends?
This selfish argument? This fire which lends
 Heat to resentment, ashes to remorse?
Canst thou bend Truth and Nature to thy will?
Bend thou, and work and wait; be strong and still;
 Soft growth is stronger than vehement force.

Be as a flower, content to be, to grow
In sweetness day by day; content to know
 The hidden blessing in the seeming curse;
A child of Love, unargumentative;
Content to be and know — as thou dost live—
 The simple secret of the Universe.

Restored

Eager for strife and struggle, Self and gain,
 And heeding not the gentle Voice of Truth,
We strive and wrestle in dark ways of pain,

And, blind and lost in passion, we disdain
  The unobtrusive Way of Love and ruth;
So live we on in sorrow and in woe,
Nor rest can find, nor blessed gladness know.

Tired of strife and anger, hate and pain,
  And weary of the wranglings of the Schools,
We turn, and look into your face again,
Beloved brother, sister; nor in vain
  Search we with purer eyes; but as in pools
Soft, deep, and silent, gaze we, finding rest;
So pass we on our way, refreshed and blest.

On releasing a captive bird

I found a little bird held fast, ensnared
  By ruthless hands; a gentle, captive prey
Thirsting for freedom, piteously scared,
  Struggling in vain to 'scape and soar away.

I marked his terror, and I took him up;
  His fluttering heart spoke out his wild despair.
"Look, you and I with the great gods shall sup
  This day," I said; then threw him into air.

Whereat he soared, and wheeled, and flew away;
  Great was his joy, and ruth - born bliss was mine;
Thus supped we both with the high gods that day;
  Thus tasted we their nectar, drank their wine.

Art thou in sorrow?

Art thou in sorrow? Art thou in despair,
  Involved in doubt and deep perplexity?
Leave thou thyself, and with thy fellows share
  The good thou hast, and thou wilt blessed be.

Let Love's bright sunshine play upon your heart;
  Come now unto your gladness, peace, and rest;
Bid the dark shades of selfishness depart,
  And now and evermore be truly blest.

When I am pure

When I am pure
I shall have solved the mystery of life,

I shall be sure,
When I am free from hatred, lust, and strife,
I am in Truth, and Truth abides in me.
I shall be safe and sane and wholly free
 When I am pure.

Immortality

He shall not die who seeks the Way of Truth;
He shall not see the corruption who doth walk
With stainless feet the Path of Purity;
He shall not wander in dark worlds of woe
Who finds the Gate of Good and enters there,
For he shall taste of immortality
While feasting at the table of his Lord.

Are you searching?

Are you searching for the happiness that does not fade away?
Are you looking for the joy that lives, and leaves no grievous
day?
Are you panting for the waterbrooks of Love, and Life, and
Peace?
Then let all dark desires depart, and selfish seeking cease.

Are you ling'ring in the paths of pain, grief-haunted, stricken
sore?
Are you wand'ring in the ways that wound your weary feet the
more?
Are you sighing for the Resting-Place where tears and sorrows
cease?
Then sacrifice the heart of self, and find the Heart of Peace.

Morning And Evening Thoughts

First Morning

In aiming at the life of blessedness, one
of the simplest beginnings to be considered,
and rightly made, is that which we all
make every day-namely, the beginning
of each day's life.

There is a sense in which every day
may be regarded as the beginning of a new
life, in which one can think, act, and live
newly, and in a wiser and better spirit.

The right beginning of the day will
be followed by a cheerfulness permeating
the household with a sunny influence,
and the tasks and duties of the day will
be undertaken in a strong and confident
spirit, and the whole day will be well lived.

First Evening

There can be no progress, no achievement,
without sacrifice, and a man's worldly
success will be in the measure that he
sacrifices his confused animal thoughts,
and fixes his mind on the development
of his plans, and the strengthening of his
resolution and self-reliance.

And the higher he lifts his thoughts,
the more manly, upright, and righteous
he becomes, the greater will be his success,
the more blessed and enduring will be his
achievements.

Second Morning

None but right acts can follow right thoughts; none but a right life can follow right acts; and by living a right life all blessedness is achieved.

Mind is the Master-power that moulds and makes.
And Man is Mind, and evermore he takes.
The Tool of thought, and, shaping what he wills,
Brings forth a thousand joys, a thousand ills;-
He thinks in secret, and it comes to pass:
Environment is but his looking-glass.

Second Evening

Calmness of mind is one of the beautiful jewels of wisdom. A man becomes calm in the measure that he understands himself as a thought-evolved being. . . .

And he as he develops a right understanding, and sees more and more clearly the internal relations of things by the action of cause and effect, he ceases to fret and fume, and worry and grieve, and remains poised, steadfast, serene.

Third Morning

To follow, under all circumstances, the highest promptings within you; to be always true to the divine self; to rely upon the inward Voice, the inward Light, and to pursue your purpose with a fearless and restful heart, believing that the future will yield unto you the need of every thought and effort; knowing that the laws of the universe can never fail, and that your own will come back to you with mathematical exactitude-this is faith and the living of faith.

Third Evening

Have a thorough understanding of your
work, and let it be your own; and as you
proceed, ever following the inward Guide,
the infallible Voice, you will pass on from
victory to victory, and will rise step by step
to higher resting-places, and your ever-
broadening outlook will gradually reveal
to you the essential beauty and purpose
of life. Self-purified, health will be yours;
self-governed, power will be yours, and all
that you do will prosper.

And I may stand where health, success,
and power
Await my coming, if, each fleeting hour,
I cling to love and patience; and abide
With stainlessness; and never step aside
From high integrity; so shall I see
At last the land of immortality.

Fourth Morning

When the tongue is well controlled and
wisely subdued; when selfish impulses and
unworthy thoughts no longer rush to the
tongue demanding utterance; when the
speech has become harmless, pure,
gracious, gentle, and purposeful, and no
word is uttered but in sincerity and
truth-then are the five steps in virtuous
speech accomplished, then is the second
great lesson in Truth learned and mastered.
Make pure thy heart, and thou wilt make
thy life
Rich, sweet and beautiful.

Fourth Evening

Having clothed himself with humility,
the first questions a man asks himself
are:-

"How am I acting towards others?"
"What am I doing to others?"
"How am I thinking of others?"
"Are my thoughts of, and acts towards
others prompted by unselfish love?"
As a man, in the silence of his soul,
asks himself these searching questions, he
will unerringly see where he has hitherto
failed.

Fifth Morning

To dwell in love always and towards all
is to live the true life, is to have Life itself.
Knowing this, the good man gives up
himself unreservedly to the Spirit of Love,
and dwells in Love towards all, contending
with none, condemning none, but loving
all.

The Christ Spirit of Love puts an
end, not only to all sin, but to all division
and contention.

Fifth Evening

When sin and self are abandoned, the heart
is restored to its imperishable Joy.

Joy comes and fills the self-emptied
heart; it abides with the peaceful; its reign
is with the pure.

Joy flees from the selfish, it deserts the
quarrelsome; it is hidden from the impure.

Joy cannot remain with the selfish; it is
wedded to Love.

Sixth Morning

In the pure heart there is no room left
where personal judgments and hatreds can
find lodgement, for it is filled to overflowing
with tenderness and love; it sees no evil,
and only as men succeed in seeing no evil

in others will they become free from sin,
and sorrow, and suffering.

If men only understood
That the heart that sins must sorrow,
That the hateful mind tomorrow
Reaps its barren harvest, weeping,
Starving, resting not, nor sleeping;
Tenderness would fill their being,
They would see with Pity's seeing
If they only understood.

Sixth Evening

To stand face to face with truth; to arrive,
after innumerable wanderings and pains, at
wisdom and bliss; not to be finally defeated
and cast out, but to ultimately triumph
over every inward foe-such is man's divine
destiny, such his glorious goal; and this,
every saint, sage, and savior has declared.

A man only begins to be a man
when he ceases to whine and revile, and
commences to search for the hidden justice
which regulates his life. And as he adapts
his mind to that regulating factor, he
ceases to accuse others as the cause of his
condition, and builds himself up in strong
and noble thoughts; ceases to kick against
circumstances, but begins to use them as
aids to his more rapid progress, and as a
means of discovering the hidden power
and possibilities within himself.

Seventh Morning

The will to evil and the will to good
Are both within thee, which wilt
thou employ?
Thou knowest what is right and what is
wrong,
Which wilt though love and foster?
which destroy?
Thou art the chooser of thy thoughts and
deeds;

Thou art the maker of thine inward state;
The power is thine to be what thou wilt be;
Thou buildest Truth and Love, or lies and
hate.

Seventh Evening

The teaching of Jesus brings men back
to the simple truth that righteousness,
or right-doing, is entirely a matter of
individual conduct, and not a mystical
something apart from a man's thoughts
and deeds.

Calmness and patience can become
habitual by first grasping, through effort,
a calm and patient thought, and then
continuously thinking it, and living in it,
until "use becomes second nature," and
anger and impatience pass away for ever.

Eighth Morning

Man is made or unmade by himself; in the
armoury of thought he forges the weapons
by which he destroys himself; he also
fashions the tools with which he builds
for himself heavenly mansions of joy and
strength and peace. By the right choice
and true application of thought man
ascends to the Divine Perfection; by the
abuse and wrong application of thought
he descends below the level of the beast.
Between these two extremes are all the
grades of character, and man is their
maker and master.

As a being of Power, Intelligence, and
Love, and the lord of his own thoughts,
man holds the key to every situation.

Eighth Evening

Whatsoever you harbour in the inmost
chambers of your heart will, sooner or later,
by the inevitable law of reaction,
shape itself in your outward life.

Every soul attracts its own, and
nothing can possibly come to it that does
not belong to it. To realize this is to
recognize the universality of Divine Law.

If thou would'st right the world,
And banish all its evils and its woes.
Make its wild places bloom,
And its drear deserts blossom as the rose-
Then right thyself.

Ninth Morning

Whatever conditions are rendering your
life burdensome, you may pass out of and
beyond them by developing and utilizing
within you the transforming power of
self-purification and self-conquest.

Before the divine radiance of a pure
heart all darkness vanishes and all clouds
melt away, and he who has conquered
self has conquered the universe.

He who sets his foot firmly upon
the path of self-conquest, who walks,
aided by the staff of faith, the highway of
self-sacrifice, will assuredly achieve the
highest prosperity, and will reap abounding
and enduring joy and bliss.

Ninth Evening

It is the silent and conquering thought-
forces which bring all things into
manifestation. The universe grew
out of thought.
To adjust all your thoughts to a perfect
and unswerving faith in the omnipotence
and supremacy of Good, is to co-operate
with that Good, and to realize within
yourself the solution and destruction
of all evil.

To mentally deny evil is not sufficient;
it must, by daily practice, be risen above

and understood. To affirm the Good
mentally is inadequate; it must, by
unswerving endeavor, be entered into
and comprehended.

Tenth Morning

Every thought you think is a force sent out.
Whatever your position in life may
be, before you can hope to enter into any
measure of success, usefulness, and power,
you must learn how to focus your thought-
forces by cultivating calmness and repose.

There is no difficulty, however great,
but will yield before a calm and purposeful
concentration of thought, and no
legitimate object but may be speedily
actualized by the intelligent use and
direction of one's soul forces.

Think good thoughts, and they will
quickly become actualized in your outward
life in the form of good conditions.

Tenth Evening

That which you would be and hope to be,
you may be now. Non-accomplishment
resides in your perpetual postponement,
and, having the power to postpone, you
also have the power to accomplish-to
perpetually accomplish: realize this truth,
and you shall be to-day, and every day,
the ideal being of whom you dreamed.

Say to yourself, "I will live in my Ideal
now; I will manifest my ideal now; I will
be my Ideal now; and all that tempts me
away from my Ideal I will not listen to;
I will listen only to the voice of my Ideal."

Eleventh Morning

Be as a flower; content to be, to grow
in sweetness day by day.

If thou would'st perfect thyself in
knowledge, perfect thyself in Love.
If thou would'st reach the Highest,
ceaselessly cultivate a loving and
compassionate heart.

To him who chooses Goodness,
sacrificing all, is given that which
is more than, and includes, all.

Eleventh Evening

The Great Law never cheats any man of
his just due.

Human life, when rightly lived,
is simple with a beautiful simplicity.

He who comprehends the utter
simplicity of life, who obeys its laws,
and does not step aside into the dark
paths and complex mazes of selfish desire,
stands where no harm can reach him.

Then there is fullness of joy,
abounding plenty, and rich and
complete blessedness.

Twelfth Morning

Every man reaps the results of his own
thoughts and deeds, and suffers for his
own wrong.

He who begins right, and continues
right, does not need to desire, and search
for felicitous results; they are already at
hand; they follow as consequences; they
are the certainties, the realities, of life.

Sweet is the rest and deep is the bliss
of him who has freed his heart from its
lusts and hatreds and dark desires.

Twelfth Evening

You are the creator of your own shadows;
you desire, and then you grieve; renounce,
and then you shall rejoice.

Of all the beautiful truths pertaining
to the soul, . . . none is more gladdening
or fruitful of divine promise and confidence
than this-that man is the master of
thought, the moulder of character, and
the maker and shaper of character,
environment, and destiny.

Thirteenth Morning

As darkness is a passing shadow, and light
is a substance that remains, so sorrow is
fleeting, but joy abides for ever. No true
thing can pass away and become lost; no
false thing can remain and be preserved.
Sorrow is false, and it cannot live; joy is
true, and it cannot die. Joy may become
hidden for a time, but it can always be
recovered; sorrow may remain for a period,
but it can be transcended and dispersed.

Do not think your sorrow will remain;
it will pass away like a cloud. Do not
believe that the torments of sin are ever
your portion; they will vanish like a
hideous nightmare. Awake! Arise! Be holy
and joyful.

Thirteenth Evening

Tribulation lasts only so long as there
remains some chaff of self which needs to
be removed. The tribulum, or threshing
machine, ceases to work when all the
grain is separated from the chaff;
and when the last impurities are
blown away from the soul,
tribulation has completed its work,
and there is no more need for it;
then abiding joy is realized.

The sole and supreme use of suffering
is to purify, to burn out all that is useless
and impure. Suffering ceases for him

who is pure. There could be no object
in burning gold after the dross had
been removed.

Fourteenth Morning

In speaking of self-control, one is easily
misunderstood. It should not be associated
with a destructive repression, but with a
constructive expression.

A man is happy, wise and great in the
measure that he controls himself; he is
wretched, foolish, and mean in the
measure that he allows his animal nature
to dominate his thoughts and actions.

he who controls himself, controls his
life, his circumstances, his destiny; and
wherever he goes he carries his happiness
with him as an abiding possession.

Renunciation precedes regeneration.
The permanent happiness which men
seek in dissipation, excitement, and
abandonment to unworthy pleasures,
is found only in the life which reverses
all this-the life of self-control.

Fourteenth Evening

Law, not confusion, is the dominating
principle in the universe; justice, not
injustice is the soul and substance of life;
and righteousness, not corruption, is the
moulding and moving force in the spiritual
government of the world. This being so,
man has but the right himself to find that
the universe is right.

When I am pure,
I shall have solved the mystery of life;
I shall be sure,
When I am free from hatred, lust and
strife,

I am in Truth, and Truth abides in me;
I shall be safe, and sane, and wholly free,
When I am pure.

Fifteenth Morning

If men only understood
That their hatred and resentment
Slays their peace and sweet contentment,
Hurts themselves, helps not another,
Does not cheer one lonely brother,
They would seek the better doing
Of good deeds which leaves no rueing-
If they only understood.

If men only understood
How Love conquers; how prevailing
Is its might, grim hate assailing;
How compassion endeth sorrow,
Maketh wise, and doth not borrow
Pain of passion, they would ever
Live in Love, in hatred never-
If they only understood.

Fifteenth Evening

The grace and beauty that were in Jesus
can be of no value to you-cannot be
understood by you-unless they are also
in you, and they can never be in you, until
you practise them, for, apart from doing,
the qualities which constitute Goodness
do not, as far as you are concerned, exist.
To adore Jesus for his good qualities is a
long step towards Truth, but to practise
those qualities is Truth itself; and he who
fully adores the perfection of another will
not rest content in his own imperfection,
but will fashion his soul after the likeness
of that other.

Therefore thou who adorest Jesus for
his divine qualities, practise those qualities
Thyself, and thou too shalt be divine.

Sixteenth Morning

Let a man realize that life in its totality proceeds from the mind, and lo, the way of blessedness is opened up to him! For he will then discover that he possesses the power to rule his mind and to fashion it in accordance with his Ideal.

So will he elect to strongly and steadfastly walk those pathways of thought and action which are altogether excellent; to him life will become beautiful and sacred; and, sooner or later, he will put to flight all evil, confusion, and suffering; for it is impossible for a man to fall short of liberation, enlightenment, and peace, who guards with unwearying diligence the gateway of his heart.

Sixteenth Evening

By constantly overcoming self, a man gains a knowledge of the subtle intricacies of his mind; and it is this divine knowledge which enables him to become established in calmness.

Without self-knowledge there can be no abiding peace of mind, and those who are carried away by tempestuous passions, cannot approach the holy place where calmness reigns.

The weak man is like one who, having mounted a fiery steed, allows it to run away with him, and carry him withersoever it wills; the strong man is like one who, having mounted the steed, governs it with a masterly hand and makes it go in whatever direction and at whatever speed he commands.

Seventeenth Morning

There is no strife, no selfishness, in the Kingdom; there is perfect harmony, equipoise, and rest.

Those who live in the Kingdom of
Love, have all their needs supplied by
the Law of Love.

As self is the root cause of all strife
And suffering, so Love is the root cause
of all peace and bliss.
Those who are at rest in the Kingdom,
do not look for happiness in any outward
possessions. They are freed from all anxiety
and trouble and, resting in Love, they are
the embodiment of happiness.

Seventeenth Evening

Let it not be supposed that the children of
The Kingdom live in ease and indolence
(these two sins are the first that have
to be eradicated when the search for the
Kingdom is entered upon); they live in a
peaceful activity; in fact, they only truly
live, for the life of self, with its train of
worries, griefs, and fears, is not real life.

The children of the Kingdom are
Known by their life, they manifest the fruits
of the Spirit-"Love, joy, peace, long-suffering,
kindness, goodness, faithfulness,
meekness, temperance, self-control"-
under all circumstances and vicissitudes.

Eighteenth Morning

The gospel of Jesus is a gospel of living and
doing. If it were not this it would not voice
the Eternal Truth. Its Temple is Purified
Conduct, the entrance-door to which is
Self-surrender. It invites men to shake off
sin, and promises, as a result, joy and
blessedness and perfect peace.

The Kingdom of Heaven is perfect
trust, perfect knowledge, perfect peace. . . .
No sin can enter therein, no self-born
Thought or deed can pass its golden gates;

no impure desire can defile its radiant robes. . . . All may enter it who will, but all must pay the price-the unconditional abandonment of self.

Eighteenth Evening

I say this-and know it to be truth-that circumstances can only affect you in so far as you allow them to do so. You are swayed by circumstances because you have not a right understanding of the nature, use, and power of thought. You believe (and upon this little word belief hang all our joys and sorrows) that outward things have the power to make or mar your life; by so doing you submit to those outward things, confess that you are their slave, and they your unconditional master. By so doing you invest them with a power which they do not of themselves possess, and you succumb, in reality not to the circumstances, but to the gloom or gladness, the fear or hope, the strength of weakness, which your thought-sphere has thrown around them.

Nineteenth Morning

If you are one of those who are praying for, and looking forward to a happier world beyond the grave, here is a message of gladness for you-you may enter into and realize that happy world now; it fills the whole universe, and it is within you, waiting for you to find, acknowledge, and possess.

Said one who understood the inner laws of Being-"When men shall say, lo here, or lo there, go not after them. The Kingdom of God is within you."

Nineteenth Evening

Heaven and hell are inward states. Sink into self and all its gratifications,

and you sink into hell; rise above self
into that state of consciousness which is
the utter denial and forgetfulness of self,
and you enter heaven.

So long as you persist in selfishly
seeking for your own personal happiness,
so long will happiness elude you, and you
will be sowing the seeds of wretchedness.
in so far as you succeed in losing yourself
in the service of others, in that measure
will happiness come to you, and you will
reap a harvest of bliss.

Twentieth Morning

Sympathy given can never be waste.

One aspect of sympathy is that of
Pity-pity for the distressed or pain-
stricken, with a desire to alleviate
or help them in their sufferings.
The world needs more of this
divine quality.

"For pity makes the world
Soft to the weak, and noble
for the strong.

Another form of sympathy is that
of rejoicing with others who are more
successful than ourselves, and though
their success were our own.

Twentieth Evening

Sweet are companionships, pleasures, and
material comforts, but they change and
fade away. Sweeter still are Purity, Wisdom,
and the knowledge of Truth, and these
never change nor fade away.

He who attained to the possession of
spiritual things can never be deprived of
his source of happiness; he will never have
to part company with it, and wherever he

goes in the whole universe, he will carry
his possessions with him. His spiritual
end will be the fulness of joy.

Twenty-First Morning

Let your heart grow and expand with ever-
broadening love, until, freed from all
hatred, and passion, and condemnation,
it embraces the whole universe with
thoughtful tenderness.

As the flower opens its petals to receive
the morning light, so open your soul more
and more to the glorious light of Truth.

Soar upward on the wings of aspiration;
be fearless and believe in the loftiest
possibilities.

Twenty-First Evening

Mind clothes itself in garments of its own
making.
Mind is the arbiter of life; it is the
creator and shaper of conditions, and the
recipient of its own results. It contains
within itself both the power to create
illusion and to perceive reality.

Mind is the infallible weaver of destiny;
thought is the thread, good and evil deeds
are the warp and woof, and the web,
woven upon the loom of life, is character.
Make pure thy heart, and thou wilt make
thy life
Rich, sweet, and beautiful, unmarred by
strife.

Twenty-Second Morning

Cherish your visions; cherish your ideals;
cherish the music that stirs in your heart,
the beauty that forms in your mind, the
Loveliness that drapes your purest thoughts,

for out of them will grow all delightful
conditions, all heavenly environment;
of these, if you will remain true to them,
your world will at last be built.

Guard well thy mind, and, noble, strong,
and free,
Nothing shall harm, disturb or conquer
thee;
For all thy foes are in thy heart and mind,
There also thy salvation thou shalt find.

Twenty-Second Evening

Dream lofty dreams, and as you dream
so shall you become. Your vision is the
promise of what you shall one day be;
your Ideal is the prophecy of what you
shall at last unveil.

The greatest achievement was at first
and for a time a dream. The oak sleeps
in the acorn; the bird waits in the egg;
and in the highest vision of the soul
a waking angel stirs.

Your circumstances may be uncongenial,
but they shall not long remain so when
you perceive an Ideal and strive to reach it.

Twenty-Third Morning

He who has conquered doubt and fear has
conquered failure. His every thought is
allied with power, and all difficulties are
bravely met and wisely overcome. His
purposes are seasonably planted, and they
bloom and bring forth fruit which does
not fall prematurely to the ground.

Thought allied fearlessly to purpose
becomes creative force: he who knows this
is ready to become something higher and
stronger than a mere bundle of wavering
thoughts and fluctuating sensations; he

who does this has become the conscious
and intelligent wielder of his mental powers.

Twenty-Third Evening

Man's true place in the Cosmos is that of
a king, not a slave, a commander under
the Law of Good, and not a helpless tool
in the region of evil.

I write for men, not for babes; for
those who are eager to learn, and earnest
to achieve; for those who will put away
(for the world's good) a petty personal
indulgence, a selfish desire, a mean
thought, and live on as though it were
not, sans craving and regret.

Man is a master. If he were not, he
could not act contrary to law.

Evil and weakness are self destructive.
The universe is girt with goodness
and strength, and it protects the good
and the strong.

The angry man is the weak man.

Twenty-Fourth Morning

Not by learning will a man triumph over
evil; not by much study will he overcome
sin and sorrow. Only by conquering
himself will he conquer evil; only by
practising righteousness will he put an
end to sorrow.

Not for the clever, nor the learned, nor
the self-confident is the Life Triumphant,
but for the pure, the virtuous and wise.
The former achieve their particular success
in life, but the latter alone achieve the
great success so invincible and complete
that even in apparent defeat it shines with
added victory.

Twenty-Fourth Evening

The true silence is not merely a silent
tongue; it is a silent mind. To merely hold
one's tongue, and yet to carry about a
disturbed and rankling mind, is no remedy
for weakness, and no source of power.

Silentness, to be powerful, must
envelop the whole mind, must permeate
every chamber of the heart; it must be
the silence of peace.

To this broad, deep, abiding silentness
a man attains only in the measure that
he conquers himself.

Twenty-Fifth Morning

By curbing his tongue, a man gains
possession of his mind.

The fool babbles, gossips, argues,
and bandies words. He glories in the fact
that he has had the last word, and has
silenced his opponent. He exults in his
own folly, is ever on the defensive, and
wastes his energies in unprofitable channels.
He is like a gardener who continues to dig
and plant in unproductive soil.

The wise man avoids idle words, gossips,
vain argument, and self-defence. He is
content to appear defeated; rejoices when
he is defeated; knowing that, having found
and removed another error in himself, he
has thereby become wiser.

Blessed is he who does not strive for
the last word.

Twenty-Fifth Evening

Desire is the craving for possession; aspiration
is the hunger of the heart for peace.

The craving for things leads ever
farther and farther from peace, and not
only ends in deprivation, but is in itself
A state of perpetual want. Until it comes
to an end, rest and satisfaction are
impossible.

The hunger for things can never be
satisfied, but the hunger for peace can,
and the satisfaction of peace is found-
is fully possessed, when all selfish desire is
abandoned. Then there is fullness of joy,
abounding plenty, and rich and complete
blessedness.

Twenty-Sixth Morning

A man will reach the Kingdom by purifying
himself, and he can only do this by
pursuing a process of self-examination
and self-analysis.

The selfishness must be discovered and
understood before it can be removed. It is
powerless to remove itself, neither will it pass
away of itself. Darkness ceases only when
light is introduced; so ignorance can only be
dispersed by knowledge, selfishness by love.

A man must first of all be willing to
lose himself (his self-seeking) before he
can find himself (his Divine Self). He
must realize that selfishness is not worth
clinging to, that it is a master altogether
unworthy of his service, and that divine
goodness alone is worthy to be enthroned
in his heart, as the supreme master of
his life.

Twenty-Sixth Evening

Be still, my soul, and know that peace
is thine.
Be steadfast, heart, and know that
strength divine

Belongs to thee; cease from thy turmoil, mind,
And thou the Everlasting Rest shalt find.

If a man would have peace, let him exercise the spirit of peace; if he would find Love, let him dwell in the spirit of Love; if he would escape suffering, let him cease to inflict it; if he would do noble things for humanity, let him cease to do ignoble things for himself. If he will but quarry the mine of his own soul, he shall find there all the materials for building whatsoever he will, and he shall find there also the Central Rock on which to build in safety.

Twenty-Seventh Morning

Men go after much company, and seek out new excitements, but they are not acquainted with peace; in divers paths of pleasure they search for happiness, but they do not come to rest; through divers ways of laughter and feverish delirium they wander after gladness and life, but their tears are many and grievous, and they do not escape death.

Drifting upon the ocean of life in search of selfish indulgences, men are caught in its storms, and only after many tempests and much privation do they fly to the Rock of Refuge which rests in the deep silence of their own being.

Twenty-Seventh Evening

Meditation centered upon divine realities is the very essence and soul of prayer. It is the silent reaching upward of the soul toward the Eternal.

Meditation is the intense dwelling, in thought, upon an idea or theme with

the object of thoroughly comprehending
it; and whatsoever you constantly meditate
upon, you will not only come to understand,
but will grow more and more into its
likeness, for it will become incorporated
with your very being, will become, in fact,
your very self.

If, therefore, you constantly dwell upon
that which is selfish and debasing, you will
ultimately become selfish and debased;
if you ceaselessly think upon that which
is pure and unselfish, you will surely
become pure and unselfish.

Twenty-Eighth Morning

There is no difficulty, however great, but
will yield before a calm and powerful
concentration of thought, and no
legitimate object but may be speedily
actualized by the intelligent use and
direction of one's soul forces.

Whatever your task may be,
concentrate your whole mind upon it;
throw into it all the energy of which you
are capable. The faultless completion of
small tasks, leads inevitably to larger tasks.

See to it that you rise by steady
climbing, and you will never fall.

Twenty-Eighth Evening

He who knows that Love is at the heart of
all things, and has realized the all-sufficing
power of that Love, has no room in his
heart for condemnation.

If you love people and speak of them
with praise, until they in some way
thwart you, or do something of which
you disapprove, and then you dislike them
and speak of them with dispraise, you are

not governed by the Love which is of God.
If, in your heart, you are continually
arraigning and condemning others,
selfless love is hidden from you.

Train your mind in strong, impartial,
and gentle thought; train your heart in
purity and compassion; train your tongue
to silence, and to true and stainless speech;
so shall you enter the way of holiness and
peace, and shall ultimately realize the
immortal Love.

Twenty-Ninth Morning

If you would realize true prosperity,
do not settle down, as many have done,
into the belief that if you do right
everything will go wrong. Do not allow
the word "Competition" to shake your
faith in the supremacy of righteousness.
I care not what men say about the "laws
of competition," for do not I know the
Unchangeable Law which shall one day
put them all to rout, and which puts them
to rout even now in the heart and life of
the righteous man? And knowing this
law I can contemplate all dishonesty
with undisturbed repose, for I know
where certain destruction awaits it.

Under all circumstances do that which
you believe to be right, and trust the Law;
trust the Divine Power which is immanent
in the universe, and it will never desert
you, and you will always be protected.

Twenty-Ninth Evening

Forget yourself entirely in the sorrows of
others, and in ministering to others, and
divine happiness will emancipate you from
all sorrow and suffering. "Taking the first
step with a good thought, the second with

a good word, and the third with a good deed, I entered Paradise." And you also enter Paradise by pursuing the same course.

Lose yourself in the welfare of others; forget yourself in all that you do-this is the secret of abounding happiness. Ever be on the watch to guard against selfishness and learn faithfully the divine lessons of inward sacrifice; so shall you climb the highest heights of happiness, and shall remain in the never-clouded sunshine of universal joy, clothed in the shining garment of immortality.

Thirtieth Morning

When the farmer has tilled and dressed his land and put in the seed, he knows that he has done all that he can possibly do, and that now he must trust to the elements, and wait patiently for the course of time to bring about the harvest, and that no amount of expectancy on his part will affect the result.

Even so, he who has realized Truth, goes forth as a sower of the seeds of goodness, purity, love, and peace, without expectancy and never looking for results, knowing that there is the Great Over-ruling Law which brings about its own harvest in due time, and which is alike the source of preservation and destruction.

Thirtieth Evening

The virtuous put a check upon themselves, and set a watch upon their passions and emotions; in this way they gain possession of the mind, and gradually acquire calmness; and as they acquire influence, power, greatness, abiding joy, and fullness and completeness of life.

He only finds peace who conquers himself, who strives, day by day, after greater self-possession, greater self-control, greater calmness of mind.

Where the calm mind is there is strength and rest, there is love and wisdom; there is one who has fought successfully innumerable battles against self, who, after long toil in secret against his own failings, has triumphed at last.

Thirty-First Morning

Sympathy bestowed increases its store in our own heart and enriches and fructifies our own life. Sympathy given is blessedness received; sympathy withheld is blessedness forfeited.

In the measure that a man increases and enlarges his sympathy so much nearer does he approach the ideal life, the perfect blessedness; and when his heart has become so mellowed that no hard, bitter, or cruel thought can enter, and detract from its permanent sweetness, then indeed is he richly and divinely blessed.

Thirty-First Evening

Sweet is the rest and deep the bliss of him who has freed his heart from its lusts and hatreds and dark desires; and he who, without any shadow of bitterness resting upon him, and looking out upon the world with boundless compassion and love, can breathe, in his inmost heart, the blessing:

Peace unto all living things,

making no exceptions or distinctions-such a man has reached that happy ending which can never be taken away, for this is the perfection of life, the fulness of peace, the consummation of perfect blessedness.

From Passion To Peace

Foreword

THE FIRST THREE PARTS of this book, *Passion, Aspiration,* and *Temptation,* represent the common human life, with its passion, pathos, and tragedy. The last three parts, *Transcendence, Beatitude,* and *Peace,* represents the Divine Life—calm, wise and beautiful—of the sage and Savior. The middle part, *Transmutation,* is the transitional stage between the two; it is the alchemic process linking the divine with the human life. Discipline, denial, and renunciation do not constitute the Divine State; they are only the means by which it is attained. The Divine Life is established in that Perfect Knowledge which bestows Perfect Peace.

James Allen

Amid the din and strife of men,
The Call Divine I hear again;
Its telling is of things apart;
Above the tumult of the heart.
High o'er where sin's dark pathways wind
Waits the wise willing of the mind;
Beyond strong Passion's guarded Gates,
There Peace awaits—there Peace awaits.

1. Passion

THE PATHWAY OF THE SAINTS and sages, the road of the wise and the pure; the highway along which the Saviors have trod, and which all Saviors to come will also walk—such is the subject of this book; such is the high and holy theme which the author briefly expounds in these pages.

Passion is the lowest level of human life. None can descend lower. In its chilling swamps and concealing darkness creep and crawl the creatures of the sunless world. Lust, hatred, anger, covetousness, pride, vanity, greed, revenge, envy, back-biting, lying, theft, deceit, treachery, cruelty, suspicion, jealousy—such are the brute forces and blind, unreasoning impulses that inhabit the underworld of passion, and roam, devouring and devoured, in the rank primeval jungles of the human mind.

There also dwell the dark shapes of remorse, pain, and suffering, and the drooping forms of grief, sorrow, and lamentation.

In this dark world the unwise live and die, not knowing the peace of purity, nor the joy of that Divine Light which forever shines above them, and for them, Yet, it shines in vain so long as it falls on unseeing eyes which look not up, but are ever bent earthward—fleshward.

But the wise look up. They are not satisfied with this passion-world. They bend their steps towards the upper world of peace, the light and the glory of which they behold, at first far off, but nearer and with ever increasing splendor as they ascend.

None can fall lower than passion, but all can rise higher. In that lowest place where further descent is impossible, all who move forward must ascend. The ascending pathway is always at hand, near, and easily accessible. It is the way of self-conquest. He has already entered it who has begun to say "nay" to his selfishness, who has begun to discipline his desires, and to control and command the unruly elements of his mind.

Passion is the archenemy of mankind, the slayer of happiness, the opposite and enemy of peace. From it proceeds all that defiles and destroys. It is the source of misery, and the promulgator of mischief and disaster.

The inner world of selfishness is rooted in ignorance—ignorance of Divine Law, of Divine Goodness; ignorance of the Pure Way and the Peaceful Path. Passion is dark, and it thrives and flourishes in spiritual darkness. It cannot enter the regions of spiritual light. In the enlightened mind the darkness of ignorance is destroyed; in the pure heart there is no place for passion.

Passion in all its forms is a mental thirst, a fever, a torturing unrest. As a fire consumes a magnificent building, reducing it to a heap of unsightly ashes, so are men consumed by the flames of passions, and their deeds and works fall and perish.

If one would find peace, he must come out of passion. The wise man subdues his passions, the foolish man is subdued by them. The seeker for wisdom begins by turning his back on folly. The lover of peace enters the way which leads thereto, and with every step he takes he leaves further below and behind him the dark dwelling place of passion and despair.

The first step towards the heights of wisdom and peace is to understand the darkness and misery of selfishness, and when that is understood, the overcoming of it—the coming out of it—will follow.

Selfishness, or passion, not only subsists in the gross forms of greed and glaringly ungoverned conditions of mind; it informs also every hidden thought which is subtly connected with the assumption and glorification of one's self. It is most deceiving and subtle when it prompts one to dwell upon the selfishness in others, to accuse them of it and to talk about it. The man who continually dwells upon the selfishness in others will not thus overcome his own selfishness. Not by accusing others do we come out of selfishness, but by purifying ourselves.

The way from passion to peace is not by hurling painful charges against others, but by overcoming one's self. By eagerly striving to subdue the selfishness of others, we remain passion-bound. By patiently overcoming our own selfishness, we ascend into freedom. Only he who has conquered himself can subdue others; and he subdues them, not by passion, but by love.

The foolish man accuses others and justifies himself; but he who is becoming wise justifies others and accuses himself. The way from passion to peace is not in the outer world of people; it is in the inner world of thoughts; it does not consist in altering the deeds of others, it consists in perfecting one's own deeds.

Frequently, the man of passion is most eager to put others right; but the man of wisdom puts himself right. If one is anxious to reform the world, let him begin by reforming himself. The reformation of self does not end with the elimination of the sensual elements only; that is its beginning. It ends only when every vain thought and selfish aim is overcome. Short of perfect purity and wisdom, there is still some form of self-slavery or folly which needs to be conquered.

Passion is at the base of the structure of life; peace is at its crown and summit. Without passion to begin with, there would be no power to work with, and no achievement to end with. Passion represents power, but power misdirected, power producing hurt instead of happiness. Its forces, while instruments of destruction in the hands of the foolish, are instruments of preservation in the hands of the wise. When curbed and concentrated and beneficially directed, they represent working energy. Passion is the flaming sword which guards the gates of Paradise. It shuts out and destroys the foolish; it admits and preserves the wise.

He is the foolish man who does not know the extent of his own ignorance; who is the slave of thoughts of self; who obeys the impulses of passion. He is the wise man who knows his own ignorance; who understands the emptiness of selfish thoughts; who masters the impulses of passion.

The fool descends into deeper and deeper ignorance; the wise man ascends into higher and higher knowledge. The fool desires, suffers, and dies. The wise man aspires, rejoices, and lives.

With mind intent on wisdom and mental gaze raised upward, the spiritual warrior perceives the upward way, and fixes his attention upon the heights of Peace.

2. Aspiration

WITH THE CLEAR PERCEPTION of one's own ignorance comes the desire for enlightenment, and thus in the heart is born Aspiration, the rapture of the saints.

On the wings of aspiration man rises from earth to heaven, from ignorance to knowledge, from the under darkness to the upper light. Without it he remains a groveling animal, earthly, sensual, unenlightened, and uninspired.

Aspiration is the longing for heavenly things—for righteousness, compassion, purity, love—as distinguished from desire, which is the longing for earthly things—for selfish possessions, personal dominance, low pleasures, and sensual gratifications.

As a bird deprived of its wings cannot soar, so a man without aspiration cannot rise above his surroundings and become master of his animal inclinations. He is the slave of passions, is subject to others, and is carried hither and thither by the changing current of events.

For one to begin to aspire means that he is dissatisfied with his low status, and is aiming at a higher condition. It is a sure sign that he is aroused out of his lethargic sleep of animality, and has become conscious of nobler attainments and a fuller life.

Aspiration makes all things possible. It opens the way to advancement. Even the highest state of perfection conceivable it brings near and makes real and possible; for that which can be conceived can be achieved.

Aspiration is the twin angel to inspiration. It unlocks the gates of joy. Singing accompanies soaring. Music, poetry, prophecy, and all high and holy instruments are at last placed in the hands of those whose aspirations flag not, whose spirit does not fail.

So long as animal conditions taste sweet to a man, he cannot aspire; he is already satisfied. But when their sweetness turns to bitterness, then in his sorrow he thinks of nobler things. When he is deprived of earthly joy, he aspires to the joy which is heavenly. It is when impurity turns to suffering that purity is sought. Truly aspiration rises, phoenix-like, from the dead ashes of repentance, but on its powerful pinions man can reach the heaven of heavens.

The man of aspiration has entered the way which ends in peace, and surely he will reach that end if he neither stays nor turns back. If he constantly renews his mind with glimpses of the heavenly vision, he will reach the heavenly state.

Man attains in the measure that he aspires. His longing to be is the gauge of what he can be. To fix the mind is to foreordain the achievement. As man can experience and know all low things, so he can experience and know all high things. As he has become human, so can he become divine. The turning of the mind in high and divine directions is the sole and needful task.

What is impurity but the impure thoughts of the thinker? What is purity but the pure thoughts of the thinker? One man does not do the thinking of another. Each man is pure or impure of himself alone.

If a man thinks, "It is through others, or circumstances, or heredity that I am impure," how can he hope to overcome his errors? Such a thought will check all holy aspirations and bind him to the slavery of passion.

When a man fully perceives that his errors and impurities are his own, that they are generated and fostered by himself, that he alone is responsible for them, then he will aspire to overcome them. The way of attainment will be opened up to him, and he will see from where and to what destination he is traveling.

The man of passion sees no straight path before him, and behind him is all fog and gloom. He seizes the pleasure of the moment and does not strive for understanding or think of wisdom. His way is confused, turbulent, and troubled, and his heart is far from peace.

The man of aspiration sees before him the pathway up the heavenly heights, and behind him are the circuitous routes of passion up which he has hitherto blindly groped. Striving for understanding, and his mind set on wisdom, his way is clear, and his heart already experiences a foretaste of the final peace.

Men of passion strive mightily to achieve little things—things which speedily perish, and, in the place where they were, leave nothing to be remembered.

Men of aspiration strive with equal might to achieve great things—things of virtue, of knowledge, of wisdom, which do not perish, but stand as monuments of inspiration for the uplifting of humankind.

As the merchant achieves worldly success by persistent exertion, so the saint achieves spiritual success by aspiration and endeavor. One becomes a merchant, the other a saint, by the particular direction in which his mental energy is guided.

When the rapture of aspiration touches the mind, it at once refines it, and the dross of its impurities begins to fall away. While aspiration holds the mind, no impurity can enter it, for the impure and the pure cannot at the same moment occupy the thought. But the effort of aspiration is at first spasmatic and short-lived. The mind falls back into its habitual error, and must be constantly renewed.

The lover of the pure life renews his mind daily with the invigorating glow of aspiration. He rises early, and fortifies his mind with strong thoughts and strenuous endeavor. He knows that the mind is of such a nature that it cannot remain for a moment unoccupied, and that if it is not held and guided by high thoughts and pure aspirations, it will assuredly he enslaved and misguided by low thoughts and base desires.

Aspiration can be fed, fostered, and strengthened by daily habit, just as is desire. It can be sought, and admitted into the mind as a divine guide, or it can be neglected and shut out. To retire for a short time each day to some quiet spot, preferably in the open air, and there call up the energies of the mind in surging waves of holy rapture, is to prepare the mind for great spiritual victories and destinies of divine import. For such a rapture is the preparation for wisdom and the prelude to peace.

Before the mind can contemplate pure things it must be lifted up to them, it must rise above impure things; and aspiration is the instrument by which this is accomplished. By its aid the mind soars swiftly and surely into heavenly places, and begins to experience divine things. It begins to accumulate wisdom, and to learn to guide itself by an ever-increasing measure of the divine light of pure knowledge.

To thirst for righteousness; to hunger for the pure life; to rise in holy rapture on the wings of angelic aspiration—this is the right road to wisdom. This is the right striving for peace. This is the right beginning of the way divine.

3. Temptation

ASPIRATION CAN CARRY a man into heaven, but to remain there, he must learn to conform his entire mind to the heavenly conditions. To this end temptation works.

Temptation is the reversion, in thought, from purity to passion. It is going back from aspiration to desire. It threatens aspiration until the point is reached where desire is quenched in the waters of pure knowledge and calm thought.

In the early stages of aspiration, temptation is subtle and powerful, and is regarded as an enemy; but it is only an enemy in the sense that the one tempted is his own enemy. In the sense that it is the revealer of weakness and impurity, it is a friend, a necessary factor in spiritual training. It is, indeed, an accompaniment of the effort to overcome evil and apprehend good. To be successfully conquered, the evil in a man must come to the surface and present itself, and it is in temptation that the evil hidden in the heart stands revealed and exposed.

That which temptation appeals to and arouses is unconquered desire, and temptation will again and again assail a man until he has lifted himself above the lusting impulses. Temptation is an appeal to the impure. That which is pure cannot be subject to temptation.

Temptation waylays the man of aspiration until he touches the region of the divine consciousness, and beyond that border temptation cannot follow him. It is when a man begins to aspire that he begins to be tempted. Aspiration rouses up all the latent good and evil, in order that the man may be fully revealed to himself, for a man cannot overcome himself unless he fully knows himself.

It can scarcely be said of the merely animal man that he is tempted, for the very presence of temptation means that there is a striving for a purer state. Animal desire and gratification is the normal condition of the man who has not yet risen into aspiration. He wishes for nothing more, nothing better, than his sensual enjoyments, and is, for the present, satisfied. Such a man cannot be tempted to fall, for he has not yet risen.

The presence of aspiration signifies that a man has taken one step, at least, upward, and is therefore capable of being drawn back. This backward attraction is called temptation. The allurements of temptation subsist in the impure thoughts and downward desires of the heart. The object of temptation is powerless to attract when the heart no longer lusts for it. The stronghold of temptation is within a man, not without; and until a man realizes this, the period of temptation will be prolonged.

While a man continues to run away from outward objects, under the delusion that temptation subsists entirely in them, and does not attack and purge away his impure imaginings, his temptations will increase, and his falls will be many and grievous. When a man clearly perceives that the evil is within and not without, then his progress will be rapid, his temptations will decrease, and the final overcoming of all temptation will be well within the range of his spiritual vision.

Temptation is torment. It is not an abiding condition, but is a passage from a lower condition to a higher. The fullness and perfection of life is bliss, not torment. Temptation accompanies weakness and defeat, but a man is destined for strength and victory. The presence of torment is the signal to rise and conquer. The man of persistent and ever renewed aspiration does not allow himself to think that temptation cannot be overcome. He is determined to be master of himself. Resignation to evil is an acknowledgment of defeat. It signifies that the battle against self is abandoned; that good is denied; that evil is made supreme.

As the energetic man of business is not daunted by difficulties but studies how to overcome them, so the man of ceaseless aspiration is not crushed into submission by temptations, but meditates how he may fortify his mind. For the tempter is like a coward: he only creeps in at weak and unguarded points.

The tempted one should study thoughtfully the nature and meaning of temptation, for until it is known it cannot be overcome. A wise general, before attacking the opposing force, studies the tactics of his enemy. Likewise, he who is to overcome temptation must understand how it arises in his own darkness and error, and must study, by introspection and meditation, how to disperse the darkness and supplant error by truth.

The stronger a man's passions, the fiercer will be his temptations; the deeper his selfishness, the more subtle his temptations; the more pronounced his vanity, the more flattering and deceptive his temptations.

A man must know himself if he is to know the truth. He must not shrink from any revelation which will expose his error. On the contrary, he must welcome such revelations as aids to that self-knowledge which is the handmaid of self-conquest.

The man who cannot endure to have his errors and shortcomings brought to the surface and made known, but tries to hide them, is unfit to walk the highway of truth. He is not properly equipped to battle with and overcome temptation. He who cannot fearlessly face his lower nature, cannot climb the rugged heights of renunciation.

Let the tempted one know this: that he himself is both tempter and tempted; that all his enemies are within; that the flatterers which seduce, the taunts which stab, and the flames which burn, all spring from that inner region of ignorance and error in which he has hitherto lived. Knowing this, let him be assured of complete victory over evil. When he is sorely tempted, let him not mourn, therefore, but let him rejoice in that his strength is tried and his weaknesses exposed. For he who truly knows and humbly acknowledges his weakness will not be slow in setting about the acquisition of strength.

Foolish men blame others for their lapses and sins, but let the truth-lover blame only himself. Let him acknowledge his complete responsibility for his own conduct and not say, when he falls, this thing, or such and such a circumstance, or that man was to blame. For the most which others can do is to afford an opportunity for our own good or evil to manifest itself. They cannot make us good or evil.

Temptation is at first sore, grievous, and hard to be borne, and subtle and persistent is the assailant. But if the tempted one is firm and courageous, and does not give way, he will gradually subdue his spiritual enemy, and will finally triumph in the knowledge of good.

The adverse one is compounded of a man's own lust, selfishness, and pride. When these are put away, evil is seen to be naught, and good is revealed in all-victorious splendor.

4. Transmutation

MIDWAY BETWEEN the hell of Passion and the heaven of Peace is the purgatory of Transmutation—not a speculative purgatory beyond the grave, but a real purgatory in the human heart. In its separating and purifying fire the base metal of error is sifted away, and only the clarified gold of truth remains.

When temptation has culminated in sorrow and deep perplexity, then the tempted one, strenuously striving for deliverance, finds that his moral servitude is entirely from himself. Instead of fighting against outer circumstances, he must alter inner conditions. The fight against outer things is necessary at the start. It is the only course which can be adopted at the first, because of the prevailing ignorance of mental causation. But it never, of itself, brings about emancipation. What it does bring about is the knowledge of the mental cause of temptation. This knowledge of the mental cause of temptation leads to the transmutation of thought, and the transmutation of thought leads to deliverance from the bondage of error.

The preliminary fighting is a necessary stage in spiritual development, just as the crying and kicking of a helpless babe is necessary to its growth. But as the crying and kicking is not needed beyond the infant stage, so the fierce struggling with, and falling under, temptation ends when the knowledge of mental transmutation is acquired.

The truly wise man, he who is enlightened concerning the source and cause of temptation, does not fight against outward allurements—he abandons all desire for them. Thus, they cease to be allurements, and the power of temptation is destroyed at its source. But this abandonment of unholy desire is not a final process. It is the beginning of a regenerative and transforming power which, when patiently employed, leads to the clear and cloudless heights of spiritual enlightenment.

Spiritual transmutation consists of an entire reversal of the ordinary self-seeking attitude of mind toward people and things, and this reversal brings about an entirely new set of experiences.

Thus the desire for a certain pleasure is abandoned, cut off at its source, and not allowed to have any place in the consciousness. But the mental force which that desire represented is not annihilated, it is transferred to a higher region of thought, transmuted into a purer form of energy. The law of conservation of energy prevails universally in the mind as it does in matter, and the force shut off in lower directions is liberated in higher realms of spiritual activity.

Along the Saintly Way towards the divine life, the midway region of Transmutation is the Country of Sacrifice, the Plain of Renunciation. Old passions, old ambitions and thoughts, are cast away and abandoned, but only to reappear in some more beautiful, more permanent, more eternally satisfying form.

Valuable jewels, long guarded and cherished, when thrown tearfully into the melting pot, are remolded into new and more perfect adornments. Likewise, the spiritual alchemist, at first reluctant to part company with long-cherished thoughts and habits, at last gives them up to discover, a little later, to his joy, that they come back to him in the form of new facilities, rarer powers and purer joys—spiritual jewels newly polished, beautiful, and resplendent.

In transmuting his mind from evil to good, a man comes to distinguish more and more clearly between error and Truth, and so distinguishing, he ceases to be swayed and prompted by outward things and by the actions and attitudes of others. Instead, he acts from his knowledge of truth. First acknowledging his errors, and then confronting them with a searching mind and a humble heart, he subdues, conquers, and transmutes them.

The early stage of transmutation is painful but brief, for the pain is soon transformed into pure spiritual joy, the brevity of the pain being measured by the intelligence and energy with which the process is pursued.

While a man thinks that the cause of his pain is in the attitude of others, he will not pass beyond it. But when he perceives that its cause is in himself, then he will pass beyond it into joy.

The unenlightened man allows himself to be disturbed, wounded, and overthrown by what he regards as the wrong attitude of others towards him. This is because the same wrong attitude is in himself. He, indeed, doles out to them, in return, the same actions, regarding as right in himself that which is wrong in others. Slander is given for slander, hatred for hatred, anger for anger. This is the action and reaction of evil. It is the clash of selfishness with selfishness. It is only the self, or selfish elements, within a man that can be aroused by the evil in another. The Truth, or divine characteristics, in a man cannot be approached by that evil, much less can it be disturbed and overthrown by it.

It is the conversion, or complete reversal of this self or selfishness into Truth that constitutes Transmutation. The enlightened man has abandoned the delusion that the evil in others has power to hurt and subdue him, and he has grasped the profound truth that he is only overthrown by the evil in himself. He therefore ceases to blame others for his sins and sufferings, and applies himself to purifying his own heart. In this reversal of his mental attitude, he transmutes the lower selfish forces into the higher moral attributes. The base ore of error is cast into the fire of sacrifice, and there comes forth the pure gold of Truth.

Such a man stands firm and unmoved when assailed by outward things. He is self's master, not its slave. He has ceased to identify himself with the impulses of passion, and has identified himself with Truth. He has overcome evil, and has become merged in Good. He knows both error and Truth, and has abandoned error and brought himself into harmony with Truth. He returns good for evil. The more he is assailed by evil from without, the greater is his opportunity of manifesting the good from within.

That which supremely differentiates the fool from the wise man is this—that the fool meets passion with passion, hatred with hatred, and returns evil for evil; whereas the wise man meets passion with peace, hatred with love, and returns good for evil.

Men inflict suffering upon themselves through the active instrumentality of their own unpurified nature. They rise into perfect peace in the measure that they purify their hearts. The mental energy which men waste in pursuing dark passions is all-sufficient to enable them to reach the highest wisdom when it is turned in the right direction.

As water, when transmuted into steam, becomes a new, more definite and wide reaching power, so passion, when transmuted into intellectual and moral force, becomes a new life, a new power for the accomplishment of high and unfailing purposes.

Mental forces, like molecular, have their opposite poles or modes of action. Where the negative pole is, there also is the positive. Where ignorance is, wisdom is possible. Where passion abounds, peace awaits. Where there is much suffering, much bliss is near. Sorrow is the negation of joy; sin is the opposite of purity; evil is the denial of good. Where there is an opposite, there is that which is opposed. The adverse evil, in its denial of the good, testifies to its presence. The one thing needful, therefore, is the turning around from the negative to the positive; the conversion of the heart from impure desires to pure aspirations; the transmutation of passional forces into moral powers.

The wise purify their thoughts. They turn from bad deeds and do good deeds. They put error behind them and approach Truth. Thus do they rise above the allurements of sin, above the torments of temptation, above the dark world of sorrow, and enter the Divine Consciousness, the Transcendent Life.

5. Transcendence

WHEN A MAN PASSES from the dark stage of temptation to the more enlightened stage of transmutation, he has become a saint. A saint is one who perceives the need for self-purification, who understands the way of self-purification, and who has entered that way and is engaged in perfecting himself.

But there comes a time in the process of transmutation when, with the decrease of evil and the accumulation of good, there dawns in the mind a new vision, a new consciousness, a new man. When this is reached, the saint has become a sage; he has passed from the human life to the divine life. He is "born again," and there begins for him a new round of experiences. He wields a new power; a new universe opens out before his spiritual gaze. This is the stage of transcendence. This I call the Transcendent Life.

When there is no more consciousness of sin; when anxiety and doubt, and grief and sorrow, are ended; when lust and animosity, and anger and envy, no more possess the thoughts; when there remains in the mind no vestige of blame towards others for one's own condition, and when all conditions are seen to be good because they are the result of causes, so that no event can afflict the mind, then Transcendence is attained. Then the limited personality is outgrown, and the divine life is known; evil is transcended, and Good is all-in-all.

The divine consciousness is not an intensification of the human; it is a new form of consciousness. It springs from the old, but it is not a continuance of it. Born of the lower life of sin and sorrow, after a period of painful torment, it yet transcends that life and has no part in it, just as the perfect flower transcends the seed from which it sprang.

As passion is the keynote of the self-life, so serenity is the keynote of the transcendent life. Rising into it, man is lifted above disharmony and disturbance. When Perfect Good is realized and known, not as an opinion or an idea, but as an experience or a possession, then calm vision is acquired, and tranquil joy abides through all hardships.

The Transcendent Life is ruled, not by passions, but by principles. It is founded not upon fleeting impulses, but upon abiding laws. In its clear atmosphere the orderly sequence of all things is revealed, so that there is seen to be no room for sorrow, anxiety, or regret.

While men are involved in the passions of self, they burden themselves with cares, and trouble themselves over many things. Above all else, they trouble over their own little, burdened, pain-stricken personality, being anxious for its fleeting pleasures, for its protection and preservation, and for its eternal safety and continuance. Now in the life that is wise and good all this is transcended. Personal interests are replaced by universal purposes, and all cares, troubles, and anxieties concerning the pleasure and the fate of the personality are dispelled like the feverish dreams of a night.

Passion is blind and ignorant. It sees and knows only its own gratification. Self recognizes no law; its object is to get and to enjoy. The getting is a graduated scale varying from sensual greed, through many subtle vanities, up to the desire for a personal heaven or personal immortality, but it is self still. It is the old sensual craving coming out in a more subtle and deceptive form. It is longing for some personal delight, along with its accompanying fear that delight should be lost forever.

In the transcendent state, desire and dread are ended, and the thirst for gain and the fear of loss are things that are no more. For where the universal order is seen, and where perennial joy in that good is a normal condition, what is there left to desire? What remains to be feared?

He who has brought his entire nature into conformity and harmony with the law of righteousness, who has made his thoughts pure and his deeds blameless, has entered liberty. He has transcended darkness and mortality, and has passed into light and immortality. For the transcendent state is at first a higher order of morality, then a new form of perception, and at last a comprehensive understanding of the universal moral causation. And this morality, this vision, and this understanding constitute the new consciousness, the divine life.

The transcendent man is he who is above and beyond the dominion of self. He has transcended evil and lives in the practice and knowledge of good. He is like a man who, having long looked upon the world with darkened eyes, is now restored to sight, and sees things as they are.

Evil is an experience, and not a power. If it were an independent power in the universe, it could not be transcended by any being. But though not real as a power, it is real as a condition and an experience, for all experience is of the nature of reality. It is a state of ignorance, of undevelopment and as such it recedes and disappears before the light of knowledge, as the intellectual ignorance of a child vanishes before the gradually accumulating learning, or as darkness dissolves before the rising light.

The painful experiences of evil pass away as the new experiences of good enter into and possess the field of consciousness. And what are the new experiences of good? They are many and beautiful—such as the joyful knowledge of the freedom from sin. They are the absence of remorse and deliverance from all torments of temptation. They are ineffable joy in conditions and circumstances which formerly caused deep affliction, and imperviousness to be hurt by the actions of others. They are great patience and sweetness of character; serenity of mind under all circumstances; and emancipation from doubt, fear, and anxiety. They are freedom from all dislike, envy, and animosity, with the power to feel and act kindly towards those who see fit to constitute themselves as one's enemies or opponents. They are the divine power to give blessings for curses, and to return good for evil; a deep knowledge of the human heart, with a perception of its fundamental goodness; and insight into the law of moral causation and the mental evolution of beings, with a prophetic foresight of the sublime good that awaits humanity. Above all, they are a glad rejoicing in the limitation and impotency of evil, and in the eternal supremacy and power of good.

All these, and the calm, strong, far-reaching life that these imply and contain, are the rich experiences of the transcendent man, along with all the new and varied resources, the vast powers, the quickened abilities, and enlarged capacities that spring to life in the new consciousness.

Transcendence is surpassing virtue. Evil and good cannot dwell together. Evil must be abandoned, left behind and transcended before good is grasped and known. When good is practiced and fully comprehended, then all the afflictions of the mind are at an end. For that which is accompanied with pain and sorrow in the consciousness of evil is not so accompanied in the consciousness of good.

Whatsoever happens to the good man cannot cause him perplexity or sorrow, for he knows its cause and issue, knows the good which it is ordained to accomplish in himself, and so his mind remains happy and serene. Though the body of the good man may be bound, his mind is free. Though it be wounded and in pain, joy and peace abide within his heart.

A spiritual teacher had a pupil who was apt and earnest. After several years of learning and practice, the pupil one day offered a question for discussion which his master could not answer. After days of deep meditation, the master said to his pupil, "I cannot answer the question which you have asked. Have you any solution to offer?" Whereupon the pupil formulated a reply to the question which he had propounded. The master then said to him: "You have answered that which I could not, and henceforth neither I nor any man can instruct you, for now you are indeed instructed by truth. You have soared, like the kingly eagle, where no man can follow. Your work is now to instruct others. You are no longer the pupil, you have become the master."

In looking back on the self-life which he has transcended, the divinely enlightened man sees all the afflictions of that life as though his schoolmasters were teaching and leading him upward. And in the measure that he penetrated their meaning and lifted himself above them, they departed from him. Their mission to teach him having ended, they left him the triumphant master of the field. For the lower cannot teach the higher; ignorance cannot instruct wisdom; evil cannot enlighten good; nor can the pupil set lessons for the master. That which is transcended cannot reach up to that which transcends. Evil can only teach in its own sphere, where it is regarded as master. In the sphere of good it has no place and no authority.

The strong traveler on the highway of truth knows no such thing as resignation to evil; he knows only obedience to good. He who submits to evil, saying, "Sin cannot be overcome, and evil must be borne," thereby acknowledges that evil is his master. It is not his master to instruct him, but to bind and oppress him. The lover of good cannot also be a lover of evil, nor can he, for one moment, admit its ascendancy. He elevates and glorifies good, not evil. He loves light, not darkness.

When a man makes truth his master, he abandons error. As he transcends error, he becomes more like his master, until at last he becomes one with truth, teaching it, as a master, by his actions, and reflecting it in his life.

Transcendence is not an abnormal condition; it belongs to the orderly process of evolution. Though, as yet, few have reached it, all will come into it in the course of the ages. And he who ascends into it sins no more, sorrows no more, and is no more troubled. Good are his thoughts, good are his actions, and the good is the tranquil tenor of his way. He has conquered self, and has submitted to truth. He has mastered evil, and has comprehended good. Henceforth neither men nor books can instruct him, for he is instructed by the Supreme Good, the spirit of truth.

6. Beatitude

WHEN DIVINE GOOD is practiced, life is bliss. Bliss is the normal condition of the good man. Those outer assaults, harassments, and persecutions which bring such sufferings to others, only serve to heighten his happiness, for they cause the deep fountain of good within him to well up hi greater abundance.

To have transcendent virtue is to enjoy transcendent happiness. The beatific blessedness which Jesus holds out is promised to those having the heavenly virtues— to the merciful, the pure in heart, the peacemakers, and so on. The higher virtue does not merely and only lead to happiness; it is happiness. It is impossible for a man of transcendent virtue to be unhappy. The cause of unhappiness must be sought and found in the self-loving elements, and not in the self-sacrificing qualities. A man may have virtue, and be unhappy, but not so if he has divine virtue. Human virtue is mingled with self, and therefore, with sorrow. But from divine virtue every taint of self has been purged away, and with it every vestige of misery. One comparison will suffice to illustrate this: a man may have the courage of a lion in attack and self-defense (such courage being a human virtue), but he will not thereby be rendered supremely happy.

However, he whose courage is that of the divine kind which enables him to transcend both attack and defense, and to remain mild, serene, and lovable under attack, such a man will thereby be rendered supremely happy. Moreover, his assailant will be rendered more happy, in that a more powerful good will overcome and cast out the fierce and unhappy evil of the other. The acquisition of human virtue is a great step towards truth. But the divine way transcends it—truth lies upward and beyond.

Doing good in order to gain a personal heaven or personal immortality is human virtue, but it is not unmixed with self, and not emancipated from sorrow. In the transcendent virtues all is good, and good is all, and there is no personal or ulterior aim. Human virtue is imperfect; it is mixed with the baser, selfish elements, and needs to be transmuted. Divine virtue is unblemished and pure; it is complete and perfect in itself. And what are the transcendent virtues that embody all happiness and joy? They are:

Impartiality; the seeing so deeply into the human heart, and into human actions, that it becomes impossible to take sides with one man or one party against the other, and therefore the power to be perfectly just.

Unlimited Kindness towards all men, women, and all creatures, whether enemies or friends.

Perfect Patience at all times, in all circumstances, and under the severest trials.

Profound Humility; the total surrender of self; the judging of one's own actions as though they were the actions of another.

Stainless Purity of mind and deed. Freedom from all evil thoughts and impure imaginings.

Unbroken Calmness of mind, even in the midst of outward strife, or surrounded by the turmoil of many hardships and difficulties.

Abiding Goodness of heart; impervious to evil; returning good for evil.

Compassion; deep pity for all creatures and beings in their sufferings. Shielding the weak and helpless; and protecting, out of pity, even one's enemies from injury and slander.

Abounding Love toward all living things; rejoicing with the happy and successful, and sympathizing with the sorrowing and defeated.

Perfect Peace toward all things. Being at peace with all the world. A profound reconciliation to the Divine Order of the universe.

Such are the virtues that transcend both vice and virtue. They include all that virtue embodies, while going beyond it into divine truth. They are the fruits of innumerable efforts to achieve; the glorious gifts of him that overcomes. They constitute the ten-jeweled crown prepared for the calm brow of him who has conquered himself. With these majestic virtues is the mind of the sage adorned. By them he is eternally shielded from sin and sorrow, from harm and hurt, from trouble and turmoil. In them he abides in happiness, a blessedness, a bliss, so pure and tranquil, so deep and high, so far transcending all the fleeting excitements of self, as to be unknown and incomprehensible to the self-seeking consciousness.

The sage has conquered passion and has come to lasting peace. As the mighty mountain remains unmoved by the turbulent ocean that beats at its base, so the mind of the sage, towering in lofty virtue, remains unshaken by the tempests of passion which beat unceasingly upon the shores of life. Good and wise, he is evermore happy and serene. Transcendently virtuous, he lives in beatific bliss.

7. Peace

WHERE PASSION is, peace is not; where peace is, passion is not. To know this is to master the first letter in the divine language of perfect deeds. To know that passion and peace cannot dwell together is to be well prepared to renounce the lesser and embrace the greater.

Men pray for peace, yet cling to passion. They foster strife, yet pray for heavenly rest. This is ignorance, profound spiritual ignorance. It is not to know the first letter in the alphabet of things divine.

Hatred and love, strife and peace, cannot dwell together in the same heart. Where one is admitted as a welcome guest, the other will be turned away as an unwelcome stranger. He who despises another will be despised by others. He who opposes his fellow man will himself be resisted. He should not be surprised, and mourn, that men are divided. He should know that he is propagating strife. He should understand his lack of peace. He is brave who conquers another; but he who conquers himself is supremely noble. He who is victorious over another may, in turn, be defeated; but he who overcomes himself will never be subdued.

By the way of self-conquest is Perfect Peace achieved. Man cannot understand it, cannot approach it, until he sees the supreme necessity of turning away from the fierce fighting of things without, and entering the noble warfare against evils within. He who has realized that the enemy of the world is within, and not without; that his own ungoverned thoughts are the source of confusion and strife; that his own unchastened desires are the violators of his peace, and of the peace of the world; such a man is already on the Saintly Way. If a man has conquered lust and anger, hatred and pride, selfishness and greed, he has conquered the world. He has slain the enemies of peace, and peace remains with him. Peace does not fight; is not partisan; has no blatant voice. The triumph of peace is an unassailable silence.

He who is overcome by force is not thereby overcome in his heart; he may be a greater enemy than before. But he who is overcome by the spirit of peace is thereby changed at heart. He that was an enemy has become a friend. Force and strife work upon the passions and fears, but love and peace reach and reform the heart. The pure-hearted and wise have peace in their hearts. It enters into their actions; they apply it in their lives. It is more powerful than strife; it conquers where force would fail. Its wings shield the righteous. Under its protection, the harmless are not harmed. It affords a secure shelter from the heat of selfish struggle. It is a refuge for the defeated, a tent for the lost, and a temple for the pure.

Where peace is practiced, and possessed, and known, then sin and remorse, grasping and disappointment, craving and temptation, desiring and grieving—all the turbulence and torment of the mind—are left behind in the dark sphere of the self to which they belong, and beyond which they cannot go.

Beyond where these dark shadows move, the radiant Plains of Divine Beatitude bask in Eternal Light, and to these, the traveler on the High and Holy Way comes in due time. From the blinding swamps of passion, through the thorny forests of many vanities, across the arid deserts of doubt and despair, he travels on, not turning back nor straying his course. He ever moves toward his sublime destination, until at last he comes, a humble and lowly, yet strong and radiant conqueror, to the beautiful City of Peace.